CASSANDRA

Cassandra

Niight Shades

J. M. Anton

Half Appy Press

Copyright © 2016 J.M. ANTON

The moral right of the author has been asserted.

All rights reserved.
No part of this publication may be reproduced, stored in a retrieval system, or transmitted, in any form or by any means, without the prior permission in writing of the publisher, nor be otherwise circulated in any form of binding or cover other than that in which it is published and without a similar condition including this condition being imposed on the subsequent purchaser.

This book is a work of fiction. Places, events, and situations in this book are purely fictional and any resemblance to actual persons, living or dead is coincidental.

Published by Half Appy Press

ISBN: 978-0-9962645-2-5

Typesetting services by BOOKOW.COM

Acknowledgments

Thank you to my daughter Pat for helping me shape up the first draft. The completion of this novel wouldn't have been possible without the support of my family and a few dedicated Beta Readers.

Thanks to Jody for two proofreads over the past several years. A big hug is in order for my editor Adele Brinkley, and for my daughter Kellie as well as my husband for reading and checking my final revision.

Prologue

Colorado 1985

Kathryn knew that her silence to protect her family was for naught as the pickup rammed them for a second time. Melinda's warning echoed in her mind: "Watch your back, Kat, and keep your kids close. He has his sights set on the on the Governor's Mansion and is systematically eliminating witnesses to past indiscretions who could stand in his way." Kathryn's on again–off again friend had issued that warning mere days prior to fleeing to her family's home in Virginia. Mel was pregnant with her third child, and feared for its safety. She'd taken her sons with her, but he'd stalked them down and taken the boys back. Kathryn wondered if he would murder his own wife for destroying his political aspirations. She also feared that he would blame her for Melinda's defection.

She was brought back to their immediate danger when Bill sped up a bit more, following a vicious bump from the cowcatcher attached to the front of the truck. There was an emergency pull off about a quarter of a mile ahead on the steep downgrade, and Kathryn was beginning to doubt they would make it. She prayed for her small daughter at home in the care of Rosa Ortez and her two young sons riding in the seat behind her.

Treetops flashed in her peripheral vision as the passenger side of the Wagoneer scraped, with an earsplitting noise, along the insubstantial guardrail. That flimsy barrier was all that kept them from leaving the bend in the road and plunging off the mountain.

The boys had dozed off, but the last jolt from behind woke them. Kathryn smiled and tried to sound calm as she gazed into their terrified eyes. "I love you," she told them for the last time. Bill overcorrected to keep the Jeep from plunging over the side. One more whack from the pickup sent them spinning directly into the path of an oncoming delivery van. Kathryn took the sound of screeching tires, crunching metal, shattering glass, and the cries of her sons into the afterlife.

Pete had a lousy day, so he stopped off for a few beers after his last delivery. He hated this job almost as much as he hated Colorado and the damned mountains, but he couldn't talk his wife into returning to Illinois. His day was going from bad to worse, and now the piece of crap truck was wheezing and sputtering up the steep grade. Only one more curve in the road, and then it was downhill from there, he thought.

Two vehicles caught his attention. A one-ton dually rammed the blue station wagon, spinning it around right in front of him! Pete stood on the brakes; he down shifted the lumbering clunker, but the driver of the blue vehicle was going too fast when he collided with Pete.

Pete Dugan was charged with DUI. He was also cited as the driver who caused the accident, and served several years in lockup on an involuntary manslaughter conviction. Never mind that he was on his side of the road. The cries of the small broken bodies in the second seat haunted him. Nobody wanted to hear about the white pickup. He recognized the logo on the truck as it squeezed past the wreckage. Pete vowed revenge on the driver of that deathmobile; the driver's cold, evil countenance would forever be etched in his memory.

An Excerpt from Cassandra:

JD escorted Gram to the car, and she entered the Italian restaurant on his arm. Casey walked behind the pair. Gram really seemed to enjoy herself, and it was obvious she was getting a kick out of parading around on JD's arm. Heck, why not? Casey figured it had probably been a long time since Gram had such a good looking man, one who wasn't gray, pay so much attention to her.

As for the other ogling females, Casey thought that they should get a load of him in his dress blues. That sight would have folks running for the defibrillators to restore the victims' regular heartbeats. Casey decided she was in the safest spot, behind him and temporarily out of range of his piercing blue eyes. The small parade, led by the hostess, ended at a secluded corner table, which suited Casey just fine. While JD was occupied seating Gram as if he were the reincarnation of Sir Galahad, Casey positioned herself in the corner and tried to fade into the shadows of the dimly lit room.

She wished she was able to relax and enjoy the evening, but she did not trust him. She was losing the daylong battle to subdue the tormenting ache behind her eyes as well as persistent nausea. Her order of minestrone soup and salad set both of her dinner companions on her case. Nibbling on a breadstick and sipping a warm cup of tea, she ignored them and surveyed the coming and going of diners.

Soup was served, and she felt that she had made an excellent choice: it was not disagreeing with her touchy stomach. She focused on her bowl and avoided eye contact as she listened to JD banter with Gram. Still, she could feel his eyes whenever they traveled her way and lingered. Hearing her name, she raised her eyes to meet two familiar faces.

Andy and Alice greeted Casey and her grandmother, who then introduced Jimmy.

Gram insisted that the couple join them. Casey moved over to the vacant chair next to Gram, leaving two unoccupied. Andy, no fool, seated Alice next to Casey, and placed himself between JD and Alice. Casey's sense of humor kicked in at the obvious manipulation.

She was digging into the pocket on her sundress for her vibrating cell while the newcomers placed their order. Casey asked Gram if she wanted to speak with Millie.

"You know that I can't hear on those contraptions. Just ask her what she wants."

"She says that she'll pick you up at nine in the morning."

"Tell her that I will be ready." Gram waved her hand in dismissal.

Casey thought her grandmother's hearing was getting worse. In addition to her lapses in memory, and her occasional bouts of believing Casey was still a child, Gram seemed to get confused and disorientated more lately. It was worrisome to Casey that getting her grandmother to a doctor's office depended on her state of mind and mood when it was time to keep the appointment.

"Millie, she'll be ready, but there is a small snag. Gram has company from out of town. Do you have room for one more on the bus tour? Wonderful! I'll pass on the good news. Oh, don't worry, you'll like him, all the ladies do."

"Okay, Gram you're all set, and you are welcome to bring Jimmy along." A small triumphant laugh escaped before she could squelch it. She didn't look at him as she tucked her phone back into her pocket, but she could feel his blue eyes burning holes through her like two powerful lasers.

"Did you just book him a seat on a senior bus tour?" Alice whispered while covertly glancing at JD.

"Yep. Sure did," she declared, and grinned at him when Alice broke out in a fit of giggles.

Andy spoiled the whole effect by bringing up her plans for tomorrow. "I was surprised to see you here, Casey. I thought Andi told me that you were going to the dispersal? Andy hovered right around six foot and had the same black curls that so frustrated his sister. His dark eyes were always serious, and the direct opposite of his sister's mischievous twinkle in her like colored orbs. Casey always wondered what possessed their mother to call her son Andrew and then name her daughter Andrea. Both were called Andy. They all grew up together and it sometimes got confusing when Casey would call for Andi.

"I had some work to clean up. I'm driving down in the morning."

"I suppose that the two of you troublemakers will terrorize every male on the premises."

"Andy, I'm crushed. You know my heart belongs to you. When Alice gets tired of your sorry butt, I'll be waiting in the wings." Casey gave him an evil little grin and winked at him. Excusing herself, she strolled to the restroom with Alice hot on her heels.

Casey took her time, washed her hands, played with her hair, and applied fresh lip-stain while Alice fired a barrage of questions at her.

"Who is he?"

Casey gave her the spiel about JD being a friend of Gram's.

3

"He's gorgeous, and those intense blue eyes. Wow!"

She decided not to comment on Alice's critique, or mention the fact that he had affected her much the same way the first time that she'd met him.

"Where is he from? What does he do?" she prodded.

"I guess he is originally from Colorado, but he is in the Marine Corps and is stationed east somewhere. Now can we drop the subject?"

"Sure. Only explain to me why he keeps looking at you like you're dessert?"

"Alice, you're letting your imagination run amok. There's nothing between JD and me, nor will there ever be."

Evidently, JD and Gram had ordered dessert while Casey was playing twenty questions with Alice. A slice of cheesecake was plunked in front of her before she finished her salad. Casey whispered to Alice, "dessert," when cheesecake was served to Gram and apple cobbler à la mode was placed in front of JD. Andy's girlfriend went into another fit of giggles that earned Casey a round of scowls. She did serious damage to the cheesecake and shrugged off Gram's disapproving scowl.

Chapter 1 (Part One)

Casey immediately zeroed in on the clutter of newspapers scattered over the front stoop as she made the turn into the drive. She tossed several days' worth of postal deliveries along with the weathered collection of news journals onto the passenger seat; she rolled the car forward to the side entrance of the little Cape Cod that she shared with her grandmother.

My God! The house was unlocked. A quick search through the interior for Gram proved fruitless. She thumbed through the calendar in her grandmother's room. Tuesday was penciled in for the North Olmsted Senior Center. Tension that had been building since she first noticed the condition of the front porch slowly began to melt away. She was always uneasy whenever her job required her to leave home for extended periods of time, and made a point of checking in with her grandmother daily. The changes in her grandmother that had developed over the past year were subtle at first. At times she was absent minded—little things like forgetting the mail, or what day of the week it was—and occasionally she dozed off in the middle of a conversation.

Casey rolled her shoulders to relieve the ache from a collision with a hotel room desk chair during the pre-dawn hours that morning. At her stoic best, it was difficult to ignore the persistent pain in her left hip and leg. She washed down couple of aspirin tablets with a tall glass of cool water.

Gram was out with friends, so she turned her attention to the tasks at hand. After tossing the neglected mail on the table, she made her way back out through the small, functional, kitchen, zipping her jacket as she went through the Dutch door that separated three stairs from the small landing at the side entry. The same entry provided access to the basement, and the half door had been added to keep the young child she had been from tumbling down the stairs. The entry and usually spotless kitchen tile were tracked with mud and outdoor debris. The muddy shoeprints, so obvious as she went back out to unload her luggage, had gone unnoticed in her near panic at the state of the littered front entry.

Her red Yukon safely parked in the detached garage, Casey tackled the small mountain of postal deliveries that had built up in her absence. She blew out a breath while gingerly easing her bruised frame onto a chair at the kitchen table. The only way I can make sense of this, she thought, is to prioritize. First sort the overwhelming mess into categories: one stack for bills, another for correspondence, and the trash can for junk mail. Organization had never been her strong suit, but Gram had nagged and scolded her over the years until it had sunk in. Stubborn as Casey was, she'd learned the value of a system in order to get unpleasant chores out of her way quickly.

Her smile returned as she sorted through the correspondence; the majority of items were birthday cards for her grandmother. Gram enjoyed an active and varied social life. Tomorrow would be a celebration of her eighty-second birthday.

Casey was interrupted from her task by several short toots coming from the drive. She exited the side door to check on the disturbance; a vehicle from the post office was idling just short of the front door walkway. She stood rooted to the concrete and stared at the thick envelope she'd signed for.

She tossed it on the small kitchen table where she'd been sorting through the mail. After removing her jacket and hanging it over the back of her chair, she made a cup of tea. As she moved through these mundane tasks, Casey kept a wary eye on the manila envelope. It wasn't as if she thought it was a letter bomb or something laced with anthrax, but she couldn't shake the persistent sense of foreboding that had overtaken her as soon as she'd touched it. Her cup of tea safely on the table next to her, she finished sorting the everyday mail. Then she cautiously opened the large envelope with the Denver postmark.

"My God!" She reread the letter from Jackson, Vosar and Day. She'd not been warned a letter like this could one day appear. Shocked and disbelieving, she tried to control the nausea taking hold of her.

Casey had always believed she'd been orphaned before her fifth birthday, compliments of a drunk driver who had taken out the rest of her family. Her impressions had always been that the accident fatalities included her father, but according to this missive from his attorneys, he had only passed from this world a few days previously, on May 11, 2006! Hair prickled at the nape of her neck. A chill that began to penetrate her bones and had little to do with the cool weather.

Last Thursday! He'd passed away last Thursday, the same night her sleep was rudely halted by a bad dream. She'd woken trembling, with tears running down her face; feeling lost and alone, she'd turned to Mark for comfort. Casey still couldn't recall the dream or nightmare; however, she did remember parts of a dream from the three subsequent nights. It was the same dream, no variation, night after night. She must have called out to her nightshade in her sleep, and that had set Mark off on his "other man" scenario.

He is standing with the setting sun at his back, and close enough for her to hear him whisper her name. She feels drawn to him, somehow she knows him. She reaches out to him as he approaches her. Light is fading when a larger dark figure casts a shadow over them. Instead of reaching for her, he places his hands in the back pockets of his jeans, lowers his head, and backs away. She calls out to him, but he shakes his head and continues to back away until he fades into the night.

Unnerved by the letter as well as her recollection of the mysterious shadow man of her dream, she suddenly craved some fresh air. Casey locked up the house and began a leisurely walk down familiar sidewalks. Sections of concrete slabs were broken and heaved from the ravages of time and invasive tree roots. The years had taken a toll along the walks where she'd learned to ride a bike and skate. She strolled around the block to the elementary school as she recalled memories of growing up in this neighborhood. Her wandering took her up the school drive and around to the playground. It was deserted this time of day. The children were in their classrooms diligently counting the minutes until the dismissal bell, much as she'd done nearly two decades earlier.

She gazed at the back of Gram's little house while she swayed gently on one of the swings. The blacktopped play yard butted up to Gram's backyard fence. Casey recalled the many years she'd spent in that house. As far back as her memory could reach, Gram had been her only family and the person she could turn to in a time of crisis.

A painful sense of betrayal bubbled up inside her and began to war with an equal dose of anger. She noticed a little blue Honda pull up to the side door she had entered only two hours earlier. Gram alighted from the vehicle. Casey decided against entering from the back gate that led into the fenced yard midway between the garage and the west property line. Still working on controlling her volatile temper, she rose slowly from the swing. Casey retraced her path and took the longer route from Maple Ridge School back home to bide some time. It surprised her to find the Honda still parked in the drive when she returned. She sucked in fortifying gulp of oxygen, squared her shoulders, and attempted to paste on a smile before entering the house.

Her grandmother and Millie cordially greeted her when she entered the kitchen. Casey politely declined the invitation to join them for lunch. Her escape was managed only because she claimed to have already eaten, but she did accept some hot cocoa. Her numb fingers warmed some as she clutched the mug in both hands. Casey anticipated the warmth of the cocoa as she made her way to her room upstairs.

The impending confrontation was not something she wished to have in front of her grandmother's friend. Casey worked by rote at unpacking her small suitcase and her carry-on. She felt a storm brewing between her ears. Warmed a bit by the cocoa, she kicked off her shoes, stretched out across her bed, and pulled a multicolored quilt around her shivering body. She listened to the muffled voices in the kitchen and silently wept. All these years she had a father, one she thought was dead. Gram must have known, but not once had she ever hinted that he was alive.

******

The musical tones of her phone woke her. After wiggling out of her cocoon, she retrieved it from the rear pocket of her jeans. She flipped it open, listened to the voicemail message, deleted it, and stuffed the phone back into her pocket. She couldn't deal with Mark at the moment.

Her clothing hit the floor in the small bath adjoining her room; the warm shower soothed her body. Hopefully, a blow dryer and a quick touch with the curling iron would help raise her sagging spirits. After slipping on a gray sweatshirt and a clean pair of jeans, Casey padded down the stairs in her stocking feet.

Gram was setting the table for supper when she entered the kitchen. Mouthwatering aromas, rich and wonderful, assaulted her senses as she descended the stairs. Casey hoped the homemade chicken noodle soup would help alleviate the cold, empty feeling that persisted at her core.

She pitched in to slice the freshly baked French bread, breathing in the yeasty scent as she carved the loaf. The teakettle began to shriek. Steam rose from the ceramic teapot, and the bags sizzled under the boiling water she poured into the vessel.

"I wasn't expecting you home until Friday, Casey."

"I wanted to be home for your birthday, so I left a few days early."

Casey flipped through her mental files. She was positive she had made it clear to Mark when they planned the trip to Vegas that she intended to be back home by the sixteenth of May. As usual lately, he either ignored or forgot about her schedule. He'd become belligerent and argumentative when she held her ground. It had been such a relief to be back home—until the earth shattering afternoon letter bomb.

Casey cleared the table, refilled their teacups, and then seated herself once more. She pulled the folded envelope from her back pocket to place it on the table in front of her grandmother. Apprehension crossed Gram's face and her hands trembled as she opened the envelope. Joan read the letter from Bill Hoffman's attorneys; she read every word, assimilating the information. A plane reservation was included with the handwritten note from Robert Jackson.

May 12, 2006
Dear Miss Hoffman,
It is with deepest regret that I must inform you of the untimely passing of your father, William G. Hoffman.

Mrs. William G. Hoffman and William's other children reside in the Portland, Oregon area. They have agreed to be here on Tuesday, May 23, 2006 at 10:00 a.m. for the reading of William's will.

Enclosed is a round trip ticket from Cleveland Hopkins International Airport to Denver. Please advise me if you are unable to make the scheduled flight.

I have been a friend of your father's for many years and I am looking forward to meeting you, in person.

Sincerely,

Robert Jackson

Joan folded the official letter, the handwritten note, and the printout of the electronic ticket, put them back into the envelope, and handed it back to Casey. Then she broached the touchy subject that she'd been dreading for years. "What are you going to do?"

"That depends on what you tell me."

"It is complicated, Casey."

"Simplify it. Tell me the truth for a change. Why was I kept in the dark about my father's survival?"

The anger in Casey's voice was understandable. Joan had hoped that Bill would show up in person one day, and she would be able to avoid the need for this talk. She began in a shaky, somewhat feeble voice.

"At first, your father wasn't expected to live. He was in the hospital for a long time and underwent multiple surgeries. You were only five and traumatized by the loss of your family. I assume that Bill didn't want you to suffer through the heartache all over again should he die from his injuries. I lost track of him when you were eight. Since then the only contact I've had has been with Robert Jackson. Checks came monthly, routed through Jackson. Until you turned twenty, your father faithfully sent extra funds for your birthday and at Christmas. I asked repeatedly for him to contact us, but he never did."

Casey rose then, and Joan's fingers tightened reflectively on the china teacup; her blue eyes, faded with age, followed her granddaughter's every move. Casey looked so much like Kathryn—the same auburn hair, the same dark green eyes—but there the likeness to her mother ended. Kathryn had been even tempered and wore a perpetual smile that warmed you like the late spring sun. Casey possessed that wonderful smile too, but she seldom displayed it. Kathryn's daughter was often stubborn and could be defiant, but her most disconcerting trait was her explosive temper. Joan thought that temper was legacy from her own late husband Philip. Her granddaughter was doing an admirable job of controlling it at present.

Casey put her cup in the sink and turned to face her grandmother. Her back was pressed to the counter as if she were trying to ground herself; she crossed her arms and turned a reproachful gaze onto her grandmother.

"All these years, you've lied to me. If my father hadn't died three days ago"—Casey raised her chin and gestured to the envelope lying on the table—"If that letter hadn't come, would you have continued to lie to me? That is what you and my father have done for all these years."

"I can't say for sure, but in all probability, yes, if I thought it was best for you."

"How could thinking that my father had died along with my mother and brothers be best for me?"

"You were only a child." Joan pleaded for understanding. "You would never have understood."

"I have been an adult a long time."

"I know that, Casey, and still the revelation hurt you. If you can't try to understand now, how could you have understood as a child?"

"Do you understand his rejection of me? His refusal to visit me or let me know he was alive?"

Joan put her head into her hands and wept. In a weary, tearful, voice she answered, "No, Casey. I never understood it, so how was I to explain his behavior to you?"

Shame washed over Casey. She knelt on the floor next to Gram's chair. As tears ran unchecked, she placed her head on the older woman's lap. Casey wrapped her arms around Gram's waist and hugged her frail body, chair and all. She hadn't realized how much weight her grandmother had lost recently.

"Don't cry, Gram. You always loved me and wanted me. He put you in an impossible situation. You tried to protect me, and I love you. We will get through this the same way we have everything else for the past twenty years, together."

Gin rummy, another pot of tea, and lighter conversation filled the remainder of their evening. Casey made a Herculean effort to bank the anger building once the initial shock wore off. She read Robert Jackson's letter again after Gram retired for the night. She punched in the number on the business card for Robert Jackson and left a message accepting the plane reservations. Hopefully, he would be able to shed some light on where her father had gone after the loss of his family and explain the abandonment of his only surviving child.

Casey checked the doors and doused all but the night lights She yawned as she trudged wearily up the stairs to her room, stripped, pulled on a tattered blue T-shirt, brushed her teeth, and plugged the charger into her cell phone. Morning would be soon enough to deal with messages; she was sure there were several from Mark.

******

Casey removed blueberry muffins from the oven, and then set the baking tins on a wire rack she'd placed on the counter earlier. While they cooled, she returned to checking her e-mail. She prioritized her response to this list of messages much as she had the pile of paper that had greeted her the previous day. Clients and business messages were read first, friends second, and items of interest last. She deleted Mark along with the other junk mail.

Pale, dawn light filtered through an overcast sky, but the rain that arrived during the night had ceased. Casey hoped the weather forecast held and the sun would prevail. She hated the thought of a gloomy day for Gram's birthday.

Her grandmother was awake and moving around; Casey put on the teakettle. By the time Gram joined her in the kitchen, the warm muffins beckoned from their oval basket. Balled cantaloupe in a little Tupperware container graced the table along with the ceramic teapot and fragrant muffins. She scooped scrambled eggs onto their plates and she set one in front of Gram.

Casey could feel her grandmother's eyes tracking her as she dished out the eggs and replaced the pan on the stove before seating herself.

"Did you get any sleep?" Gram asked.

"Some. I woke early, unable to doze off again. I decided to catch up on some of my e-mail."

"I see you also baked muffins and scooped out melon balls?" If unable to climb on the back of a horse and ride off a bad mood, her granddaughter baked whenever she was upset.

"I decided to make breakfast for you today. Happy birthday, Gram."

"Thank you, dear." She wasn't sure how to broach the subject of Casey's relationship with Mark. She opted for a straightforward approach to the delicate question. "Have you and Mark parted ways?"

Casey managed a small laugh, Gram had a way of cutting to the chase. "Yeah, you could say that." She didn't want to talk about the whole debacle. At the moment, she was still feeling raw and out of sorts.

"I need to check in at the studio. Be ready at six. We're going out to celebrate your birthday."

Casey had arranged for small party at Gram's favorite restaurant as a surprise and hoped that Millie hadn't spilled the beans.

"Then you've decided to go to Denver?"

"I left a message on Robert Jackson's voice mail last night accepting the plane tickets."

Robert Jackson confirmed her fight reservations several hours later. She would be leaving Cleveland Hopkins on Sunday, May 22^n on United 4100 departing at 12:38 pm and returning from Denver the morning of May 25th. A shuttle service was available to the Radisson on Quaker Street where a room had been reserved for her.

Gram had been as surprised as Casey to be informed of the existence of her father's other family. Joan encouraged her granddaughter to make the trip.

Casey managed to surprise Gram with the party. Joan accompanied her granddaughter to dinner under the impression it would be a quiet meal, only the two of them. Tears threatened to betray Gram's stoic expression as she discovered her party was twenty strong! Most of the celebrants were very loud and bawdy senior citizens. It was a good thing Casey had reserved a private dining area, or they likely would have been asked to leave. She wondered several times during the evening if Gram's friends had always been a rowdy bunch, or had age given them freedom to do as they pleased and thumb their noses at those who may disapprove?

It was scary to think what she would be like when she reached their venerable age. It probably wouldn't be a quiet or mild-mannered person who would emerge. At nearly twenty-six, she was becoming less and less likely to compromise. She'd already resolved never again to let a man influence her behavior or her decisions. Casey's take me for what I am or leave me alone attitude had only strengthened over the past ten days.

Still, she wished she had a little more time to compose herself before her impending trip to Denver. Her father had left her behind. He'd made a new life for himself and had embraced a new family. She was mad as hell.

Chapter 2

She would have driven under other circumstances, but time would not allow that luxury. Casey was physically and emotionally exhausted. She was finding it a challenge to analyze her decision to make the trip to Denver. She speculated that her impending trip was curiosity about her father or her half-brother and the woman who had taken her mother's place in his life. Then the thought occurred to her that maybe the whole jaunt across the country was only an escape to put off another confrontation with Mark.

Casey took a deep breath as the big-bodied jet taxied onto the runway; she avoided flying whenever possible. She hated long lines, frequent delays, the lack of control, and traveling with strangers. She closed her eyes and silently repeated the Lord's Prayer as the plane gained enough speed for liftoff.

Lake Erie greeted her when she slowly lifted her eyelids. The window seat provided a spectacular view of the Cleveland skyline as the jet circled and gained altitude. Robert Jackson had booked a direct flight, and she wouldn't have to go through the takeoff and landing process more than once today. She was thankful for that small blessing. Once the plane was airborne, she began to relax.

Casey covertly eyed the passenger seated next to her. She was grateful that he was occupied with his laptop and seemed oblivious to those around him. She closed her eyes and pretended to sleep. The similarities to Mark were unnerving. The man wore a similar expensive navy suit and an identical pastel blue shirt, open at the collar. She would bet her last dollar there was a red tie in the pocket of his suit coat. Italian loafers encased his long, narrow feet, a Rolex decorated his left wrist, and not one hair on his head was out of place; he even wore the same citrus scent that Mark preferred. The clone next to her made her queasy as the memory of their first encounter played in her mind.

A mutual friend's birthday party in April of 2004 was the first time she met Mark Anderson, and they'd dated off and on during that spring and early summer. He'd pleaded with her to accompany him to his family's annual Independence Day celebration. In hindsight, it was the biggest mistake of her life. She was still dealing with the repercussions from that July fourth. He'd sent her flowers, called her just to say hello, and they had dinner several times a week. Theater tickets, concert tickets, and tickets to ball games—he was always coming up with a couple of tickets for this or that. She was not used to all the attention. She'd made a superhuman effort to banish her irritation at his disruption of her work schedule and her time at home with Gram. Ironically, it was Gram who'd insisted she needed more of a social life. Gram didn't count the friends she rode with at Bonnie's stable or her meetings and dinners with clients as being social.

Casey had to admit that he was good company most of the time, and she usually enjoyed herself when they went out together. She decided the bulk of her problem was lack of practice in assimilating someone else into her life and hectic schedule. She'd determined to be more agreeable. He'd sprung a proposal on her last Christmas. The shock must have been written all over her face. As a result of her obvious reticence, he was quick to assure her that long engagements were a tradition in his family.

Their relationship gradually changed following the engagement. He demanded more of her time and became petulant if she had other plans or obligations. He either couldn't, or wouldn't, understand the demands of her work or the need to complete a commissioned project on time. Often, she had to meet with clients over dinner as well as during what Mark considered, regular work hours. The third degree got old quickly. "Where have you been and with whom?"

Her biggest mistake was probably sleeping with him. She'd been unmoved and wanted more than anything merely to escape his presence, afterward. Her habit had become to vacate whatever bed they shared as soon as he was sound asleep, and that had been almost as soon as he'd rolled off of her.

It was hard to explain why she was unmoved by Mark's advances. A brief fling in high school had been her first experience. She and her partner had grown up together, and the intimacy was the first time for both of them. For all their fumbling inexperience, the sex had been sweeter and more intense than what had transpired between two consenting adults in Mark's bed.

Her only other encounter had been with a young math tutor during her junior year of college. The union had been pleasant, but nothing to brag about.

Casey figured she was incapable of romantic feelings and had capitulated when Mark apologized for his insensitive behavior. He had suggested they get away for two weeks together without the stress of work and conflicting schedules. She'd supplied him with several dates that would work for her, and he agreed to apply for time off around one of those dates. Instead, he made reservations to

Las Vegas for the night of the fifth of May through the nineteenth. She hadn't bothered to argue with him. She merely changed her return ticket for the morning of the sixteenth.

An amplified voice announcing their arrival time at Denver International startled her. She must have dozed off!

******

After dumping her luggage unceremoniously on the floor, she called home.

Gram would fret until she heard Casey had arrived safely. "Hey, I'm here." Her grandmother seemed to have been surprised by the call. She frowned at the display on her cell as the call ended.

She walked over to the desk and reached for the house phone. It rang when she put her fingers on it to lift the receiver; the sound scared the bejeezus out of her. She took several deep breaths and reached for the receiver again with the same hand she had just snatched back. Her heart was still pounding like a war drum when she heard the mysterious Robert Jackson welcome her to Denver and inform her that they had reservations at seven. He would meet her in the lobby at six twenty. Not six thirty, but six twenty! Casey had a few clients who scheduled their time in minutes; their hourly rates were usually astronomical. How could her father afford to hire a high-priced law firm like Jackson, Vosar, and Day? The firm was paying her plane fare and the pricey hotel accommodations. Shuttle service to and from the airport was also included.

Casey drew back the sheer white curtains covering the window that dominated the outside wall. She marveled at the view. Trees obscured homes, businesses, and roads in the immediate foreground. The magnificent backdrop of mountains dwarfed the partial view of the Denver skyline, abundant with high-rise buildings.

The snowcapped mountains appeared various shades of muted blue and lavender. Was it the time of day, or atmospheric conditions? Whatever the cause, the effect was dramatic and breathtaking.

She wished she had taken the time to pack her camera and lenses. She made use of the photo function on her cell, sending the visual note to her e-mail, and then turned her attention to unpacking.

The plain unassuming woman who had flown into Denver was shelved, along with the running shoes, jeans, T-shirt, denim jacket, and ponytail. Her choice of travel attire served its purpose. No one had paid the least bit attention to her or tried to engage her in conversation. She assessed the reflection staring back at her and thought the woman in the mirror looked confident and business like, but with a touch of femininity. She approved of the tailored navy skirt that fitted her snugly through the hips, ending slightly above her knees. A nude shade of nylons and navy pumps matching her leather shoulder bag were understated but flattering. Casey adjusted the chain on a small heart-shaped locket so that it rested slightly above her breasts; it was a striking contrast to the white turtleneck, and matched her gold ear studs. She kept jewelry to a minimum. The only other items she wore were a gold watch and a large gold clip that held her auburn hair back away from her face. Her makeup was subtle, and her nails were clear polished. She pulled on a navy blazer and checked her bag for the electronic room key before heading down to the lobby.

Her watch, adjusted to Mountain Time, read 6:15 pm when she reached the lobby. She wandered around, taking in the atrium and the rest of the décor. She also did a little people watching. Casey knew who he was as soon as Robert Jackson entered. She'd researched him following the receipt of the infamous letter, but his pictures did not prepare her for the man. He was tall and slender, but built like a runner, still fit, and an impressive looking man of fifty-something. He wore an expensive looking western cut blue suit and black boots. She glanced at her watch as he entered: six-twenty on the dot.

Maybe it was perverse, but she waited for him to go to the desk and request that she be informed of his arrival. He'd walked right past her, and she wondered why he hadn't recognized her. She knew he had received photos of her from Gram. Priceless was the only way to describe his slack-jawed expression when she sidled up alongside him and proceeded to inform him that Miss Hoffman was no longer in her room. Sticking out her hand, she introduced herself. He shook the offered hand while looking her over like she was an apparition. He recovered quickly and smiled at the mischievous glint in her eyes.

"My pleasure, Miss Hoffman. Please call me Bob."

"Agreed, Bob, if you drop the Miss Hoffman routine and call me Casey."

Bob grinned, offered her his left arm, and escorted her out the door.

On the ride over to the restaurant, he admitted that he hadn't recognized her. "The last photo I'd seen of you was taken in your high school cap and gown, seven years ago. Mrs. Curtis stopped sending me photos after that."

Casey didn't reply, but she thought that Gram had probably given up trying to convince her father he had a daughter worth knowing.

They arrived at precisely seven and were seated immediately. Bob was amused at the interaction between Casey and their waiter, who was taking their drink order. Casey ordered a Colorado Bulldog, and then asked the waiter if he knew what that was. The young man was affronted; he informed her that he knew well what the drink was, adding, in an indignant voice, "After all, this is Colorado."

When Casey ordered the buffalo steak Bob gave her a skeptical look before he ordered trout. She admitted that she'd never tasted buffalo. "That's the reason I ordered it."

"You do have an adventurous spirit!"

His comment made Casey wonder if she would regret her order. The evening was not proceeding very well. First she managed to alienate the waiter, which seemed to strike Mr. Jackson's funny bone. Now, her dinner order appeared a source of amusement. Evidently, she was not the person he'd expected.

The rolls and salad had barely arrived when Bob let out an audible groan. "Casey, say nothing without consulting your attorney."

She bluntly informed him, "I don't have an attorney."

"Do you have a dollar bill?" he asked, staring over her left shoulder.

She dug her wallet out of her bag, pulled out a likeness of George Washington, and handed it to him.

"Miss Huffman, you've retained my services for the duration of the evening. We will take care of the formalities, at my office, in the morning. Don't answer any questions about your father or any plans you may have for the future without consulting me."

Casey thought that was a strange request since the whole purpose of this meeting was to cover many of the aforementioned topics. Also, there was this other family of her father's that she wanted to discuss. A deep, booming voice halted the question on the tip of her tongue as the large male form it belonged to came into the peripheral of her sight. It took all the self-discipline she could muster not to take Jackson to task when he told the overbearing person, by the name of Big Joe Gannon, that he didn't mind at all if he and JD joined them for dinner.

"Casey, this is your nearest neighbor, Joe Gannon."

Casey merely nodded as she was introduced. She glanced over her shoulder in the direction he'd arrived, but she didn't see anyone else.

Big Joe noted her searching for his dinner companion, "I'm havin' dinner with my little brother before I drive him to the airport. JD is checkin' on flight information."

Big Joe was a large man, a couple of inches over six foot, graying brown hair, and blue-gray eyes that lacked any warmth. His physical appearance matched his huge voice. His shoulders were broad, he was a little thick around the middle, and like Bob Jackson, he also appeared to be in his mid-fifties. Casey noted his exaggerated, good old boy, Texas, drawl.

The waiter returned with two additional menus and place settings. He took their new dinner companion's drink order of scotch on the rocks, and then the waiter looked past her left shoulder and asked, "What will you have, sir?"

"Scotch, neat." JD's softly spoken baritone had more impact than that of his boisterous brother. She felt his voice vibrate through her; it was disconcerting to say the least. She'd been busy attempting to control her temper as well as assessing Big Joe and never saw their second dinner guest approach. He took the empty seat on her right, facing his brother, and Casey quickly picked up on the hostile vibes. It was obvious, to her, that there was a huge rift between the two Gannon men.

"Please accept my apologies for our intrusion, and my condolences on your loss." The new arrival turned to Bob, greeting him in the way of old friends. She guessed that Bob Jackson had invited the Gannon men to dine with them only because of his liking for the younger brother.

JD seemed to know who she was. She couldn't think of a thing to say about his condolences; how could she explain to anyone that she'd thought her father dead for twenty-one years and not known differently until ten days ago? Entranced by his deep blue eyes, she merely nodded to acknowledge his apology. Talking was probably not a viable option anyway. Lord, he was intimidating in his dress uniform. She was willing to bet that not many had the nerve to take on this Marine Captain. His hair appeared to be darker brown than that of his brother, but it was difficult to tell in the subdued light, and with his short military haircut. He also had a couple of inches in height over the older man.

Robert Jackson resumed his formal introductions when the waiter left to place their orders. Big Joe was grating on her nerves. She was not in the best of moods, and he'd been staring at her since seating himself at their table. The next words he spewed forth snapped the fragile restraints she had on her simmering temper.

"There was no need for introductions, Bob. I knew who the little lady was as soon as I saw her. She's the spitting image of Kathryn." He smiled and patted her left hand.

Casey didn't like him or his phony smile that never reached his cold, calculating eyes, so she snatched her hand away at his unwarranted physical contact.

"Mr. Gannon," she addressed him, and was promptly interrupted.

"Call me Big Joe, honey, everybody does."

Casey leveled him with a cold stare and, not totally managing to subdue her temper, she continued. "Mr. Gannon," she repeated, adding deliberate emphasis on *mister*. "My mother has been gone a long time, and I do not remember her. From all of the accounts that have been shared with me, by my grandmother, my mother was a pleasant, even-tempered, paragon of virtue, and her smile lit up the world. I may look like my mother, but the similarities end with the physical. Those who know me will attest that I'm stubborn to a fault. I'm defiant and vindictive, I hold a grudge forever, and I have a nasty temper. Also, I do not like being touched by strangers."

Captain JD Gannon filled the awkward silence that followed her rather rude set-down of his older brother. A wicked grin on his face, he lifted his glass of scotch in salute. "Gentlemen, a toast to the very lovely and fiery Cassandra Hoffman." She watched his blue eyes twinkle with suppressed laughter as he proposed the toast.

The remainder of the dinner proceeded without incident. Casey made a concerted effort to be pleasant and not lose her temper. Occasionally, she caught JD watching her as if he were expecting her to blow up again. How did he know her given name? She was tempted to ask him, but was leery of having any further conversation that might include his obnoxious brother. She decided to bank her curiosity.

On her way back from a much-needed retreat to the ladies' room following a tense dinner, she realized that the two Gannon men were taking their leave of Bob Jackson. Big Joe appeared to be in the midst of a heated discussion with Bob, and she didn't want to walk into the middle of it. She altered her course and went to the bar where she selected a stool in the corner away from the other patrons. JD seated himself on the stool next to her and ordered refills of their earlier drinks. He gave her a quelling look when she informed him that she was capable of ordering and paying for her own drink. Assuming that she'd just insulted his male ego, she found herself relenting and allowed him to pick up the tab.

She wondered how much longer his brother was going to berate Bob Jackson and decided right then and there that JD could read minds. It sure would explain some of the insightful comments and the expectant glances he shot her way whenever she was about to lose her temper.

He downed his scotch in one gulp, then stood, and grinned at her as he promised to drag his brother away from her dinner companion. Before leaving, he leaned close to her and said, "If you have any questions, after tomorrow, or need me, Bob knows how to contact me."

Casey was trying not to squirm as he bent down to speak softly so only she could hear him. She couldn't take her eyes off him as he turned, placed his cap onto his head, and then literally dragged his brother out the door. She decided that her flushing and the warmth had to be caused by the potent drink. It was left half-finished on the bar when she returned to join Jackson at their table.

******

Bob asked her what she thought of their unexpected dinner guest as he drove her back to the hotel.

She didn't think that "one gorgeous hunk with beautiful blue eyes" was the appropriate response. Giving his question some thought, she opted for, "He's a formidable man, definitely intimidating, and probably violent on occasion. He also has a strange sense of humor. How old is he?" She couldn't imagine what had made her ask that. She really had to stick to tea or water; the two drinks seemed to have pickled her brain.

"How old is who?" Bob gave her a quick glance before he returned his attention to the road.

Casey had the feeling that they were talking about two different people.

Bob chuckled, "I was referring to Big Joe."

She tried again, focusing this time on the older man. "He's wealthy, ruthless, and a bully. The man is used to getting things his way. I think he runs roughshod over anyone who gets in his path."

Bob chortled once more, "You are very astute with his character analysis."

She gleaned additional information during the discussion of their dinner companions. JD was also a client of Bob's, as well as a friend. "In my opinion, Big Joe was attempting to compliment you by comparing you to your mother. Big Joe always had a soft spot for Kathryn, and you as a child."

Her one-dollar attorney was also concerned that she may have made a powerful enemy.

On her way from the elevator to her room, she replayed the events of the evening. She had a hunch that Big Joe somehow found out where she would be this evening and that running into her hadn't been an accident.

She washed off her makeup, brushed her teeth, and pulled on her big purple sweatshirt. After placing a wake-up call for six, she turned on the TV, and crawled under the covers. Her intention was to watch the local news and weather, but exhaustion won out, and she was sound asleep in minutes. The TV was still on when she bolted out of bed. "What the hell?"

******

Denver faded into the night as the jet engines powered the metallic bird higher into the heavens, and the pilot adjusted its heading to the east. JD stretched his long frame and eased the back of the seat to a more comfortable position before closing his eyes. He let his mind drift over the day's events.

Big Joe had ulterior motives behind his insistence that he, instead of Hector Ramirez, drive JD to Denver. Instinct had told him there was more to the dinner invitation than the mending of fences between the two of them, as his elder claimed. He'd questioned Big

Joe's choice of The Restaurant 1515 as opposed to something at or nearer the airport. It was hard to ignore the itch between his shoulder blades whenever he was in his elder's company, and JD made a point not to expose his back to Big Joe.

The son of a bitch had used him to ambush Bob Jackson and Bill Hoffman's little girl. Big Joe had eyes and minions throughout the state and well beyond. Years of power brokering had put a lot of important and connected people in his debt. One of his informants must've shared the location and time of Jackson's reservations. JD knew as soon as he'd entered and seen his brother seated at a table with Jackson the full extent of the ruse. Her auburn hair was a dead giveaway.

He'd slowed his pace as he approached the table, inhaled deeply, and then let his breath out slowly; he schooled his countenance in order to give nothing away to his sibling when he met the grown-up version of the little girl from his past. Still, he was unprepared for the impact! His gut clenched, and he had to struggle for a normal voice. Big Joe was, for once, correct. She looked like her mother. It also appeared that Casey hadn't appreciated the observation. JD made a mental note to remember that; he didn't want to fall into the trap that had brought down her wrath upon Big Joe.

Cassandra Hoffman's green eyes flashed when her temper was up, and she still lifted her chin with the defiance of a prizefighter daring her antagonist to bring it on. Bill had shared pictures of her, over the years, as well as letters from her grandmother that had been routed through Bob Jackson. She was ten in the last photo he'd seen of her before Bill remarried and left Philips County for a new life in Portland.

Tomorrow was going to be a rough day for her. Not only was she meeting Bill's new wife and children, but also she would find out about him.

JD hoped she would contact him before he deployed again. Bill's will aside, he didn't want to lose track of her once more. He'd forgotten how close he'd always felt to her, when they were children, until he gazed once again into her eyes. The connection was still there! He felt as if a huge missing piece from the puzzle that was his life had suddenly fallen into place.

Chapter 3

The loud ringing of the phone yanked Casey back just as she was reaching for him with the intention of halting his retreat. "What the hell?" she grumbled. Her hands shook with the residual effects of her dream as she fumbled with the handset and croaked out a sleepy response. The cheerful voice on the other end wished her a good morning and informed her that this was her 6:00 am wake-up call. What an annoying person, she thought, and wondered how anyone could be that cheerful in the morning. Casey tried to recall her quickly fading dream. She closed her eyes, searching for an instant replay. It was no use; the nightshades were gone. Once more she wondered if the ghosts that haunted her sleep were visions of the future or specters firmly rooted in her past.

She stepped out of the shower and took stock of her reflection in the steamy mirror. "Prioritize," she advised her reflection.

"Breakfast first." Perhaps a good strong cup of coffee, from the courtesy pot, would give her a bit of a jumpstart.

Bob was sending a car for her at nine. There was plenty of time to order a quick breakfast from room service.

Next, wrinkles needed to be removed from her black suit and gray silk blouse; the outfit hadn't traveled well. She was cutting it close. Her watch showed that it was three minutes till nine. One last minute chore: switch the contents of her navy bag to the black leather shoulder bag she would be using for the day. She assessed the overall look. The hem of the black-on-black pinstriped slacks brushed the top of soft black leather pumps that matched the shoulder bag. The dove gray silk blouse was simple with a V neckline. She wore no jewelry other than her watch. Casey donned a suit jacket that matched her slacks, placed the strap of her bag over her left shoulder, and entered the elevator at 9:05 am.

She'd expected someone from the law firm—an assistant, a paralegal, an intern—but what she got was a professional chauffeur and a white limo. He didn't show any indication of being annoyed by her late arrival and was handling the traffic jam with equal aplomb. He introduced himself as Ken, opened the door for her and informed her that he would be her driver for the day. Ken looked to be in his late forties, slightly built, a bit under six foot, salt and pepper hair, brown eyes, and a warm smile.

Rush hour in Denver was every bit as aggravating as rush hour in Cleveland. It was a frustrating fact of life everywhere that people needed to commute to a central work place. Traffic was at a standstill.

She overheard Ken call ahead to apprise Mr. Jackson, "We're tied up in traffic, and will arrive later than anticipated."

It sounded as if he were talking to someone other than Bob. Casey hoped the message would be relayed to him. As the thought flitted through her mind she gazed out at the passing cars and trucks also crawling along. Except for occasional glimpses of the majestic mountains, they could be stuck in traffic anywhere. The interstates were all the same and fairly uninteresting, especially within city limits. Casey found her mind wandering back to dinner the previous evening and her very brief encounter with Captain JD Gannon. She wondered where he was this morning. He'd been on his way to the airport when he left them, but that was all she knew. Well… not quite all—she knew that she could reach him through Bob Jackson, but she wasn't sure she liked the feeling that he knew more of what was going on than she did. She couldn't shake the idea that she should somehow remember him.

Finally, they reached their destination. Her nerves were already raw when she entered the elevator. As the doors began to close, a teenage boy thrust his arm through the gap, and they sprang back open. Casey watched him with a good deal of suspicion when he leaned against the frame of the elevator opening to keep the doors from closing. He grinned at her as he crossed his arms over his chest and turned his attention toward the lobby. Three stunning women entered the elevator.

Great, she thought, I'm trapped in an alien transport on my way to an alternate universe where all the women are tall, blonde, and have baby blues. Or maybe, I've been cast in one of those films marketed to little girls that star the Barbie icon and her frien*ds*. The three were at least five foot ten, and—with the exception of the variation in age—they could have been cast from the same mold. The trio was regal, sophisticated, and aloof. Casey was sure the perfume they were wearing was every bit as expensive as their outfits, but she was fighting nausea from the scent within the close confines. The senior Barbie's designer skirt hit about mid-knee; her navy-colored suit and pale blue silk blouse looked high end. The outfit probably cost more than Casey made in two weeks.

Aesthetically, she found the elevator hijacker a relief and a welcome contrast to the blondes with the heart-shaped faces and aristocratic airs. Nearly as tall as the women, he appeared to be in his early teens, that awkward, gangly, time of life. An engaging smile set off a mischievous twinkle in his hazel eyes. Outrageously long lashes and eyebrows of a slightly darker brown than his wavy hair enhanced those appealing eyes. His high cheekbones, square jaw, and a patrician nose with a sprinkling of freckles already commanded a second look. The freckles kept him from being a complete heartbreaker. She felt sorry for the teenage girls in his path; they wouldn't stand a chance.

The hijacker and the blondes exited the elevator on the sixth floor. Casey went in search of the ladies room as soon as she stepped out behind the others. The long ride from the hotel, as well as the nausea, had left her in need of a comfort stop. Necessities out of the way, she washed her hands for the third time, looked at her reflection in the wall-sized mirror, and lectured her image about procrastination. She took a deep breath, applied fresh lip-stain, gave her reflection one last pep talk, and headed for suite 680. As a result of her side trip, she entered the offices of Jackson, Vosar and Day nearly fifteen minutes after exiting the limo.

******

Bob was relieved this morning that he'd scheduled Casey to meet him at nine. He hoped to have a private conversation with her, so he'd penciled her in an hour before Susan and her family. An early morning traffic accident had delayed Casey, and—as fate would have it—Susan Hoffman arrived early. Once Susan and her children were seated in his office, Bob ordered coffee and drinks for Bill's second family. Bob left them in the care of his paralegal while he went to track down Casey. He was pacing the reception area while talking to Ken on his cell phone when she entered the office.

It was obvious that Casey hadn't expected to him to be waiting for her in the reception room. He was a little agitated when he took her by the arm and escorted her into a small conference room.

"You're late. Did you get lost?" he questioned as they sat down at the small table.

"I needed to find a restroom."

"There's a restroom here, in our office, should you have a further need." He realized that he was making her uneasy, so he sat back, took a deep breath, and relaxed. "Your father's estate is complicated, and I'd hoped to prepare you for some of the stipulations. Once again I have to ask for your patience. I promise to make everything clear and answer all your questions following the formal reading of the will. Unfortunately, it will have to wait until later since the others arrived early and are waiting for us."

"So why did you let the two Gannon men join us last night, if you had so much information to discuss with me?"

"I thought it was a unique opportunity to meet JD and Big Joe. They both had a lot to do with some of the decisions that your father had made in drafting his will."

Bob escorted her into his office and introduced her to the other family that shared her last name.

******

Casey had thought that she was prepared to meet her father's other family. She tried not to show shock, but it was a struggle not to let her preconceived dislike of her stepmother and her daughters be obvious.

Daddy's second wife was introduced as Susan Hoffman. So there they were, her father's other family, the three Barbie dolls and an elevator hijacker.

Her stepmother's skirt rose slightly above her knees as she sat with her long shapely legs crossed, blatantly assessing Casey, who likewise made a closer inspection than the brief look that she'd given the foursome in the elevator. The only thing Casey could imagine she had in common with Susan's daughters was their approximate age. Lisa appeared to be the older and possessed a superior attitude. Her pastel blue tunic enhanced her eyes. It was belted with a gold linked chain that rode low on her hips, allowing only the lower half of her navy slacks to show, and her navy heels were duplicates of the pair on her mother. Erica, the younger sister, established her independence with a sparkly white camisole that set off a light rose-colored pair of slacks. Her painted toes were a close match to the pants and peeked out of white sandals with small heels.

Casey's half-brother's name was George, and he was grinning from ear to ear. He'd already shed his gray suit coat. It was hanging on the coat rack with the black tie that he'd been wearing half hanging out of its pocket. The first two buttons on his white shirt were open, and the sleeves were rolled up slightly below his elbows. His black loafers looked new, expensive, and suspiciously like he had deliberately tried to scuff them. His enthusiastic greeting, "Howdy, Sis." had Casey involuntarily grinning back at him.

She didn't know if George had placed his lanky form strategically or if the seating arrangement was only a lucky coincidence, but she took advantage of the vacant chair on his left. His mother and sisters were seated to his right, effectively allowing Casey to use him as a buffer.

What a nightmare! The only reason she'd come was to find some answers to her abandonment by her father and satisfy her curiosity about his new family. She'd no idea that her father had been wealthy. In addition to his own accumulated wealth, he was the only son of obscenely rich parents who on their passing had left the bulk of their estate to him. Upon the death of his parents, nearly a decade before his passing, her father had used up a large portion of his inheritance setting up trust funds for his son, his adopted stepdaughters, and Casey. He'd stipulated that the trust funds could not be touched until the child owner reached the age of thirty. Casey kept her attention focused on Bob Jackson. She didn't look at anyone else, and she concentrated on maintaining the disinterested look of an impartial observer.

Her mind wandered back to the conversation with her grandmother following the arrival of the letter that brought her here. Gram had not been able to shed any light on why her father had abandoned her and insisted that he remain dead to his young daughter. She was pulled back to the present by Bob's voice; he was asking her a question. She'd wandered off somewhere in the middle of the listing of stocks and investment inventories that included real estate holdings. "I'm sorry, Mr. Jackson, what was your question?" She thought, boy, I really had zoned out!

******

Bob had been observing her attempt to control what he already knew was a quick temper, and regretted that he'd been unable to talk with her more in depth before this. He was astute at reading people; she was disinterested and had decided that this proceeding did not involve her. Her mind had taken a side road. Cautiously he asked, "Do you understand the partnership provision of the ranch?"

Casey sighed, before admitting that she wasn't paying attention. "I'm really sorry, but I was thinking of something else, and don't have a clue what you are talking about or how to answer your question."

Bob noticed George perk up. He'd been sagging in his chair, yawning, and constantly checking his watch while receiving reproachful looks from his mother. He was now wearing a devilish grin and was watching Casey intently.

"Your father," Bob began, pausing to make sure that she was with him. "In addition to the trust fund already set up, the stocks, and cash settlement, he left you a half partnership in the Colorado ranch where you were born." Her green eyes were radiating vivid sparks, and her chin elevated defiantly. He knew she was about to explode, so he tried to head her off. "Casey, I will discuss the particulars of the partnership arrangement with you later this evening, but be assured this is a substantial bequeathal." He watched her as she rose and picked up her shoulder bag as if preparing to leave. "Casey, we aren't quite finished yet."

"I am. This proceeding has nothing to do with me."

"Casey, please sit back down. You promised to give me a chance to explain your father's reasoning for some of these stipulations. It was unfortunate that we were interrupted last evening, but there are some personal matters concerning you that we need to discuss."

Bob groaned when Susan obviously took objection to Casey's declaration. Using her most commanding voice, the one that probably put her children in their place, she unleashed it on Casey. "Young lady, have a little respect for your father's memory. Mind your manners, and sit back down!"

Susan's rendition of the outraged mother was impressive, but Bob knew that Casey had grown up with a woman possessed of a tongue like a razor. He also knew the sparks were about to fly when Casey closed the door she'd been about to exit and rounded on her mother's replacement. She let loose. "No." She moved closer and looked directly into Susan's baby blues. "No, I haven't any respect for my father. I've mourned him for twenty-one years along with the rest of my family. He abandoned me, as it turns out, to start a new life with three Barbie look-a-likes and to father another son. I don't want anything to do with him or his stinking bequeathals.

You can split whatever he left me among you, give it to charity, or stick it where the sun doesn't shine. Personally, I don't give a damn, Step-mommy."

Susan sat there with a shocked expression on her face as Casey turned her back on the occupants of the room to exit.

"Excuse me a moment." Bob punched the speed dial on his desk phone. "Ken, Casey Hoffman just left here. She's emotionally distraught. Please make sure that she gets safely back to the hotel."

Bob resumed the reading of Bill Hoffman's will. Following the reading, he was discussing some of the provisions with Susan when Mary, his administrative assistant, alerted him to a call on line two. Ken informed him that Casey still had not exited the main entrance. He estimated she'd stormed out of his office almost twenty minutes earlier. Where could she have disappeared?

He pressed the intercom to the reception room. "Mary, please check out the restrooms on this level and report back to me."

"What is going on with that girl?" Susan asked. Her disgust was obvious.

"Bill provided for Casey anonymously through this office. Until eight days ago, she'd been under the impression that her father died in 1985 along with her mother and brothers. I convinced her to come here by promising to fill her in on the life Bill lived after losing his family and attempt to explain his reasoning for relinquishing his small daughter. Unfortunately, Bill's old neighbor showed up at dinner last evening. I cautioned her not to say anything in front of him. I was hoping to meet with her early this morning before the reading of his will, but she was delayed in traffic and arrived later than I'd planned."

"And we were early," George commented.

******

Once out of suite 680, Casey made a mad dash for the restroom down the hall, her jacket hit the tile floor as she flung open a stall door, but she hadn't quite made it. So there she was standing at the wall dryer with wet hair, wearing only her black lace bra, and attempting to dry her blouse when her stepmother walked in. To Casey's immense relief Susan took one look at her, turned around, and retreated.

Unfortunately, she returned in a matter of minutes with reinforcements. Their entrance coincided with another dash for the toilet. When Casey returned to where she'd left her clothes and shoulder bag, Erica was using a blow dryer on Casey's gray blouse. Lisa was busy unpacking a Dunkin Donut bag, but instead of the usual fare she pulled out a toothbrush, sample size toothpaste, and mouthwash. Susan was armed with several hand towels, and a washcloth.

"Where did you get these things?" she asked. Susan had only been gone a few minutes.

Lisa was the one who supplied the answer to Casey's question, obviously enjoying tattling on her mother. "Mom raided the executive bathroom of Jackson and Associates."

Thirty minutes later, with fresh makeup, dried hair, a slightly wrinkled but dry blouse, and accompanied by the three blonde rescuers, Casey walked back into suite 680. Her stepfamily hadn't given her a choice, and they stuck to her like glue. Erica was solicitous, having come to the conclusion that Casey was pregnant because pregnant women spent a lot of time hanging out in the bathroom. "Mom was sick all the time when she was carrying George."

Lisa held the opinion that it was their company making Casey sick, and Susan felt the problem was an attack of nerves. They all looked at her as if she were a basket case or a bomb that might explode at moment.

Lunch went fairly well. Casey decided on the chicken dumpling soup. Gram always said it was good for you if you were feeling under the weather, and it seemed to work. She apologized to Susan and the others for her outburst and began praying that she wouldn't get sick again. Apologies always stuck in her throat, but it bothered her that she'd taken her anger and frustration out on Susan. After all, she'd recently lost her husband, and the others had lost their father. They were all still mourning him, and Gram would have been upset that she'd behaved so badly.

******

Susan, Lisa, and Erica were off on a shopping trip. Casey declined Susan's invitation to join them by claiming that she didn't feel up to shopping. Bob sidelined her to make the suggestion that she pick up a pair of jeans and walking shoes, unless she'd brought the items from home. George obviously wasn't looking forward to shopping with the female members of his family. His escape presented itself when he overheard Casey ask Ken if he knew of any tack shops that carried western wear. George was quick to inform them that he too wanted jeans and for them not to leave without him.

Ken made use of the time waiting for George to inquire, "What is it that you have in mind?"

"I don't want fashion plate, but functional western clothing that I can use around the barn at home." George returned with a devilish grin spread across his face. He took great pleasure informing her that he was to keep an eye on her and make sure that she didn't wander off or get lost again. She gave up trying to convince him that she hadn't been lost.

Casey felt a little self-conscious as Ken parked the limo next to the pickup trucks in the front of the unassuming shop on N. Federal.

That unease passed quickly once she stepped through the doors, and the odor that is unique to leather greeted her. She felt at home for the first time since leaving Ohio.

They spent almost two hours shopping. Casey ended up purchasing two pair of Wranglers, a tan plaid shirt, a green and blue striped shirt, and a denim jacket. She also bought a pair of water-resistant, brown boots with a rounded toe. Meanwhile, George was giving his mother's credit card a workout. He found four pairs of jeans, five shirts, a denim jacket, as well as a leather jacket. On a roll, he added two pair of boots and was now looking at the tooled leather belts. Casey was watching him sort through the belts and decided a little guidance might be in order. He'd looked at her in wide-eyed horror when she asked what look he was attempting to project. "The belt you are taken with gives a multitude of impressions. One could assume that you are a rich fellow who can flaunt tradition, or you're an urban cowboy. A bit plainer selection would declare, 'I am a westerner, a horseman, or a cowboy and have no need to impress anyone.'"

George replaced the black belt, with all the bling, so quickly that it could have been a hot potato, and Casey fought the urge to laugh out loud.

She guided him toward a soft leather belt, brown, with minimal tooling and recommended that if he wanted black, to stay simple. "You can dress up or down with a nice leather belt and get much more use out of it."

She also helped him purchase his first belt buckle, tactfully picking out a nice-size silver buckle that had a gold roped edge and a place to engrave his initials. He bought two; the second one had her initials on it. She was so touched that she splurged and bought a belt like his. His hat purchase was a hoot. Obviously he had never worn a Stetson or any other western hat. Finally, all selections were paid for. Casey returned to the fitting room; when she reemerged she wore jeans, the tan plaid shirt, denim jacket, her new brown boots, belt, and buckle. Her hair was tied back in a ponytail that peeked out the back of a denim ball cap, with a quarter horse sewn on the front in a tan thread. She'd stuffed her suit and blouse into the shopping bag.

George was so taken with her transformation that he decided to follow her lead. Casey was sure Susan was not going to be happy that he had stuffed his suit into a plastic shopping bag. Then he charmed the owner into taking a picture of the two of them using his cell phone. Casey gave him her e-mail so he could forward a copy to her.

The plan was to have Ken drive them back to their hotels. That was when she learned the others were also staying at the Radisson on Quaker Street. They were in the limo only a short time when Susan called for Ken. Traffic was already getting heavy, and the clock was approaching five, so Ken swung over to pick up the rest of George's family. Casey let out an audible groan at George's comment, "We're so busted!"

That wasn't the kind of reassurance she needed. She glared at him, but he merely grinned, shrugging his shoulders. Her stomach was rolling again. This new brother of hers had assured her that his mother and sisters would be shopping for hours, yet, and Casey had a feeling she was going to get the blame for his excessive purchases.

She'd just lied to Gram, "Oh, everything is going pretty smoothly. I have some neat photos to share with you when I get home." Casey didn't feel that she should tell Gram the truth about her meeting with Bob Jackson or her feelings about it. The revelations would only worry her. It was useless trying to relate the mixed emotions and ambiguous feelings she had for her father's second family. Maybe when she got home she would have a better handle on this confusing turn of events.

Dinner was to be down in the hotel restaurant at seven, and failing to show up was probably not an option. The tenacious blondes would most likely appear to drag her out of her room. She traded her tan shirt for a teal sweater, brushed her hair out, and let it hang around her shoulders. She stuffed her wallet in a back pocket of her jeans along with the key card and walked to the elevator with a reluctant step, much like a person walking the last mile to the gallows. Casey knew she should be relieved there hadn't been any hysterics or accusations flung her way concerning George's shopping spree. She couldn't shake the feeling, however, that the other proverbial shoe was about to drop. Bob Jackson was joining them for dinner. She was beginning to regret letting her curiosity get the better of her and making the trip to Colorado. Her life, as well as her emotions, had been in turmoil since the arrival of his letter. Whenever she met with him, things got worse.

Dinner progressed pleasantly. George and Bob Jackson kept the conversation flowing. Before calling it a night, Susan extended an invitation for Casey to visit them in Portland.

George was reluctant to end the evening, "Gee, Mom, it's early still."

"We have to pack tonight, George, and Mr. Jackson needs to spend some time with Casey before the tour in the morning."

George wanted to stay and accompany Casey to the ranch, but his mother reminded him that school was still in session and he already had a lot of work to make up. He rose from his seat, walked over to Casey, enveloped her in a huge bear hug, pecked her on the cheek, and said, "Don't be a stranger, Sis. If you don't visit me, I'll have to make my way to Ohio."

Casey wasn't a hugger, and his display of affection was as disconcerting as his devilish grin. She said a prayer of thanks that night that her father's other family was flying back to Oregon early in the morning. Then the other shoe dropped!

Bob had just asked her if she would like an after-dinner drink.

"Do I need one?"

"I recommend it."

He was right; she did need the bracer.

"How much of the information from the reading of the will did you grasp this morning, Casey?"

"My father left a bunch of money to his children, including me, but we have to turn thirty before we get it. Also, I've been honored with half ownership of the place where I was born."

"You retained more than I thought. I wish you would've stayed around for the rest of the reading."

"Well…I didn't, and I thought that my position regarding his bequeathal was crystal clear."

"I guess the best place to start is with the ranch. Bill was not sure what your reaction would be or your age when his will took effect. He left the other half to the ranch to JD Gannon."

Casey nearly choked on her swallow of the rum-enhanced fruit drink. "Captain JD Gannon who shared dinner with us last night?"

"Yes."

"Why?"

"JD had been taking care of the place when Bill was laid up or away. He has continued to care for the place and stays there when he is home. Ben Ramirez is on retainer to maintain the house, barn, and twenty surrounding acres while JD is on active duty."

"So why didn't my father leave it to JD?"

"Like I said, he had no way of knowing how old you would be when he passed. He knew that JD would see to the day-to-day operations and not let Big Joe steal it out from under you."

"In other words, JD is my babysitter," she said as she got up from the table.

"Casey, don't leave. There, are many more items that I need to discuss with you."

"Goodnight, Bob."

"I'll pick you up at ten tomorrow morning. Most of the heavy traffic will be gone by then, and it will shorten the travel time to the ranch."

She merely nodded her head, turned, and made her way to the elevator.

Casey was a reluctant participant on the planned tour. She wondered if she would recall any part of the time she'd lived there.

Chapter 4

Memories had been assaulting JD for the past two days. Instead of the reoccurring nightmares and flashbacks of multiple tours in the mid-east, it was other images from his past keeping him awake and staring toward the ceiling through the darkness. Twenty years and then some had passed since he'd last seen little Cassie. Now, the woman who called herself Casey was haunting his waking hours and inserting her curvy little body into his dreams. It annoyed him that she could so easily distract him. Distracted Marines went home in flag-draped coffins, but he couldn't shake her from his mind.

He wondered if Bill Hoffman had any idea what he had done? JD had deliberately severed ties with the remaining Gannon clan following the passing of James Gannon ten years earlier. Hector and Rosa Ramirez, along with their son Ben, ran the ranch that he'd inherited from his father. Jim Gannon was listed as his father on his birth certificate, and he had always claimed that relationship. Ugly memories inundated his restless mind. His thoughts went from pleasant memories of Cassandra Hoffman to the confrontation between him and Big Joe during the reading of Jim's will. In a rage over their father's disposition of assets, Big Joe made the astonishing claim that JD was illegitimate. His brother asserted that JD's mother, Val, was a loose woman, and JD could be his own son or that of any of a score of other men. At that point, JD had laid him out cold in the attorney's office.

Jim Gannon had structured trust funds for his grandsons, and he split the rest of the land and assets between his two sons. That bequeathal had put him on an equal footing with Big Joe.

He shook off the painful memories of his dad's death and the aftermath. JD hoped that Cassie would not be as scarred by the pending events as he feared. Would she remember the ranch or anything about her life before the accident?

******

Outside of Denver, away from the city and urban sprawl, Northeastern Colorado was arid and barren. Here and there, clumps of wild flowers struggled to lift their faces to the sun. Colorado had always brought images of mountains and ski resorts to Casey, but Northeastern Colorado was flat as a pancake, so flat that if she gazed to the east she imagined that she could see the curve of the earth as it blended with the clear blue sky. The harsh appearing landscape was a stark contrast to Ohio, with its lush foliage and thick green grass. Even the farm fields were peculiar to her; she'd noticed on her approach to Denver many of the cultivated fields appeared to be round. Circular sprinklers used for irrigating those crops were responsible for that phenomenon. Farmland in her area of the country resembled a huge calico quilt with large squares laid out across the land when viewed from the air.

Colorado was alien to Casey; she felt uneasy and out of place. She enjoyed traveling and experiencing new places, but Bob Jackson kept referring to the ranch as her home. Home was a small house on a dead end street in the Buckeye State, but she kept that to herself as she listened to him explain the lay of the land.

Nothing, absolutely nothing, was familiar. The ranch could have as easily belonged to strangers. She didn't experience any recognition; not one thing in the house or any of the outbuildings stirred long lost memories. The place was in decent repair thanks to JD and his hired caretaker. An open porch stretched the length of the southern exposure. She followed Bob across the porch and through the back door into a large open room. A scruffy tan mat covered a gray slate tile at the entry. She'd noticed a similar mat on the outside of the door, and next to it an iron boot scraper with horseshoes welded on each side to serve as its legs. Tile extended five or six feet into the room. Hardwood flooring and the stone fireplace were all that occupied what Casey assumed would have been the family room. Empty oak bookshelves flanked each side of the fireplace that was centered on the far wall. The hearth to her right was the same gray and tan slate tile that she was standing on. Narrow floor-to-ceiling windows were placed at the outside edges of the built-in bookcases. One large window looked out onto the back porch. To her left was the kitchen. It appeared small given the size of the family room. Unlike that room, it looked much like it must have twenty years earlier. Casey shook her head in disbelief; it was obvious to her the renovations had been started by a man. A woman would've begun with the outdated kitchen.

At the other end of the kitchen was a room that she assumed was a dining room. It too was empty except for an old chandelier. Further investigation uncovered a large pantry off the small kitchen. She assessed it as the easiest way for someone to remodel the kitchen.

A room at the front of the house was a study or possibly an old office space that could be accessed from the family room or from the front foyer. Pocket doors allowed the room to be closed off from the activity in the family room. Directly across the foyer from the study was a formal living room. Bob led the way down a hall separating the kitchen from the living room, and past the staircase to the master suite. This room was the only one that had furniture, if you could call it that. The furniture consisted of a king-size bed, which dominated the room, an old scarred chest with brass handles on the drawers that had turned black with age and neglect, and a well-worn leather armchair with a matching ottoman.

The thought occurred to her that this must be where JD slept whenever he was in Colorado. She shook off the speculation about JD and deliberately moved on. Off the sleeping area was another smaller room with walk-in closets. Bob identified the space as a sitting or dressing area. The master bath was unfinished but had a functional shower, commode, and washbasin. The half bath between the family room and the study had been completed.

The second floor was untouched; the three small bedrooms were as they had been when she'd lived here. Not that she remembered, but Bob's running commentary provided what her memory couldn't. It took all the self-control that she could muster to keep from running down the stairs and out of the house.

******

She stood in the yard, fists clenched and sucking in great gulps of oxygen. At first, she hadn't realized he was speaking to her. "I am sorry, Bob, but I missed the question."

"Are you all right, Casey?" Her pale face and distraction concerned him.

"I am fine. Only a bit tired."

"I asked if you would like to see the barn?" He knew from years of correspondence with Joan that Casey loved horses. She'd been riding since she was old enough to climb aboard. He wondered whether she remembered riding in front of her father, but whenever he mentioned Bill she became hostile. He'd tried to explain that Bill was never the same after the accident.

Her father had tried to come home, but he couldn't handle the memories.

"It needs a lot of work." Casey gave him a strange look. This time she'd caught him off in another place or time, but he recouped quickly.

"You've enough wherewithal at your disposal to renovate or replace to suit you, and when your thirtieth birthday rolls around you will be a wealthy woman."

"There isn't a need for me to change anything. I won't be living here. Let JD do whatever he wants with the property. He can even buy me out, cheap. I don't want anything to do with this place."

"Casey, I explained that Big Joe has a little over six years left on a thirty-year lease covering the bulk of this property. The only thing exempt is the house and twenty surrounding acres. He's the only prospective buyer at this time; no one else will make an offer with the lease hanging over the place. "

"That's JD's problem. It doesn't have anything to do with me. I'd like to go now."

******

Five days later, Bob Jackson placed a phone call to North Carolina.

"She never said another word on the trip back to Denver." He'd just brought JD up to date on the events involving the reading of the will, and Casey's reaction to Bill's other family. He walked JD through her lack of interest and declaration that he could buy her out.

"She refused to have dinner with me and checked out that night. She didn't make her early flight the next morning, so I went to check on her. I was able to track her movements through the hotel shuttle service. She took a redeye to Chicago with a two-hour layover there before boarding a plane to Cleveland."

"Did she get home safely?"

"I spoke with Joan Curtis, and she assured me that Casey is home. I don't think she's aware of the stress her granddaughter is under."

"What gives you that impression, Bob?"

"When I asked her how Casey was doing, she told me that she has been a bit upset and uncommunicative lately. In her opinion, her granddaughter's behavior is a result of a spat with her fiancé and a broken engagement. Casey let her believe that she had a wonderful time in Colorado, even sharing some photos. However, she told Joan the vacation was over, and she had a lot of work to catch up on. I've given up trying to glean any information from Joan. She doesn't seem to be aware of what transpired here and continues to evade my questions. I've repeatedly requested that Casey contact me, but she hasn't. She ignores my messages on her cell and e-mail. I'm at a loss as how to proceed with her, JD. It looks like she's dumped the whole works in your lap."

"Ben will continue to care for the place when I can't be there. In the meantime I'll make a trip to Ohio as soon as I can get a few days away from the base. I was hoping she would contact me, but it looks like I'll have to make the first move."

"Big Joe's attorney is pressuring us to let him present a purchase offer."

"Isn't he aware that neither of us can sell without the other person's consent?"

"He's aware, but he also knows she doesn't want any part of Colorado or her father's legacy, and I'm sure that Big Joe thinks he can convince you to sell."

"Keep me advised. I'll talk to you again after I get back from Ohio."

It was the second week in June before JD could take a few days' leave. Mrs. Curtis was gracious once he identified himself as Cassie's childhood friend, Jimmy Gannon. He claimed he would be in the area for a few days and would like to visit with them. He knew that he ran the risk of Cassie avoiding him, but he couldn't just drop in unannounced.

Chapter 5

Knotted shoulder muscles and a blinding, eye-watering, headache won out, so Casey closed her computer. She rolled her shoulders to relieve the stiffness and took the last bottle of water from the small fridge that sat perched on the side-by-side filing cabinets. She found a couple of ibuprofen samples in her desk drawer and let them slide down her throat along with the icy water.

Maybe I should lower the temperature control on the fridge. There isn't much in it at the moment. Musical tones derailed her train of thought. She read the digital ID screen on her cell. "Hi, Andi. What's up?"

"You know the farm that we visited last fall, the one on the other side of Mansfield?"

"Are you talking about the Quarter Horse Haven?"

"Right. They're having a big dispersal sale. Someone involved with the place took the last ride. There is information on their website. The auction starts at noon, but you can ride or watch the horses being ridden starting at eight. I'm going down with Bonnie tonight. Do you want to come along?"

"Thanks, but I think I'll drive down in the morning. Tell Bonnie to save a space in the trailer incase I find something I like. Thanks for the heads up, Andi."

She disconnected her laptop from the large monitor on her desk to place it into her bag, and was once again interrupted by an incoming call. Her headache was down to a dull roar, and she thought if it was Mark she was going to lose it by screaming the roof down. The readout showed that it was Gram.

"Hi Gram."

"Are you coming home soon, Casey?"

"I'm packing up my laptop and getting ready to lock up as we speak. Is there something you want me to pick up on the way?"

"No dear. Your young man is here, and he is taking us out to dinner."

"You tell his sorry sneaky ass that if he's still there when I get home I'm going to kick it down the steps, and call the police!" She shouted over the phone as she was sprinting out the door of her studio.

"The creep has a lot of nerve to waylay Gram like this. See how he likes spending the weekend in the slammer for harassment." she muttered.

It had been over a month since she walked out on their relationship, and her ire grew at his constant efforts to resume it. Not damn likely, she thought. Not a soul on this earth had ever hit her and got a second chance.

The fifteen-minute drive was frustrating, as all three traffic lights turned red. She piloted the Yukon into the drive way too fast. Tires screeched in protest as she floored the brakes. She hadn't spotted his BMW on the way in, but he could have parked it in the school lot and come in the back way. She stormed into the house prepared to do battle, but came to an abrupt halt. He sat at the kitchen table with Gram just like he was at home. She wanted to smack the amused grin off his face.

"I really would prefer to go peaceably, but if you are intent on kicking my backside down the steps you're welcome to try." He watched her green eyes flash, but she unclenched her fists.

"Did Gram tell you I said that?"

"No. I was sitting right here when you issued the threat to my person. Every word was quite clear."

"Your person? I never met a marine who avoided a cuss word or two."

"Have you met a lot of marines, Cassie?"

"What are you doing here, Captain Gannon?"

"Visiting a friend," he replied in a calm reasonable tone that was the direct opposite of what he was feeling. God, she was spectacular when riled up.

"We're not friends."

"We used to be friends, Cassie." There was a longing in his voice that he quickly squelched. "Actually, I was referring to your grandmother."

Snorting in disbelief, she countered, "You're going to sit there and tell me you came here only to visit with my grandmother. Do you expect me to believe that crock?"

"Casey, what is wrong with you? You're being very rude to Jimmy, and he's my guest." Gram was obviously confused by her hostility.

"Jimmy?" Casey inquired before she snorted again and broke into laughter. "He's little Jimmy? The little Jimmy who rode here from Colorado with his father to bring us home?"

"Yes dear. You were too ill to fly back with me, so Jimmy's father offered to drive us home."

Without another word she turned, walked out the door, and pulled the Yukon back toward the garage. She could feel his eyes on her as she unloaded a large carrying case and a file folder before heading back toward the house. It was like walking a gauntlet, but she went past them and started up the stairs. Then she stopped, backed down the steps, and looked over her shoulder at him. "Where's your car, Jimmy?" 'Jimmy' was spit at him in sarcastic tones that were the polar opposite of the sweet reminiscent qualities of her grandmother's voice when she used the name.

"I haven't rented one yet. I took a cab here from the airport." She gave him a skeptical look that all but called him a bald-faced liar. It was obvious she didn't buy his declaration of a simple visit with her grandmother.

"Well, I guess that means I'm driving." She gave him an evil grin.

He wondered if she planned to shove him out of the vehicle into traffic, but decided that she wouldn't do anything violent in front of her grandmother.

A few minutes passed before he heard from her again; she hollered down the steps, "Are you two about ready?"

"Fifteen minutes," they both answered at the same instant and Gram giggled. She actually giggled! Casey could not remember her grandmother ever giggling.

This time the persistent cell caught her as she entered the kitchen. The call was from her bank. That chore had gone completely out of her mind when Gram had called her, and the bank was now closing. She impatiently shifted weight from one foot to the other while she rummaged through her bag. Casey waited for the person on the other end to verify her funds and to fax the letter of credit over to her studio. Distracted, she hadn't heard JD walk back into the room. Instinctively, she backed away from him. He hadn't appeared as large and intimidating seated at the back of the kitchen table. Maybe she'd been in such an agitated state of mind that she hadn't noticed. Listening intently to the instructions on other end of the line, she was unprepared when Gram's landline rang. Heart pounding against her chest, she made a vertical leap that would have put Superman to shame. Answering her cell while blocking the entry had not been smart move. Her hasty retreat from JD had backed her up to the kitchen wall phone. The ring had all the impact of standing under the elementary school bell, unaware that it was about to deafen you.

Gram must have cranked the ring volume up as high as it could go. Her disconnected cell dangling from one hand, she turned and placed the other hand on the wall to ground herself. Forehead pressed against the cool wall, she sucked in great drafts of oxygen while trying to will her quaking body and her rampaging heart back to normal.

"Casey, answer the phone; it might be Millie about the bus tour tomorrow." Gram's muffled voice issued the order from the bathroom.

Casey lifted the receiver with a sigh of resignation. "Hello?" Could this day get much worse? she wondered. "Why are you calling here, Mark?"

JD watched her closely as she listened to the caller. He noticed the emotions play across her face and heard her voice turn hard and cold.

"Let me make this clear. I do not want your apologies, or your excuses. If you continue to harass me, I will report you as a stalker and you can deal with the police." She slammed the receiver down, adjusted the ring to a more reasonable level, and then placed her forehead against the wall and shuddered as a long sigh escaped her pursed lips.

JD wanted to touch her, hold her close. Instead, he asked. "Cassie, is there anything I can do?"

She turned to gaze into his blue eyes and chalked one more offense up to Mark. She'd made a complete ass of herself, panicked that Mark had decided to use Gram to get to her. Still, wasn't JD doing the same thing? She tabled that disturbing thought and handed him the keys to the Yukon. "You can drive. I don't feel very well. I think I forgot to eat today."

"You haven't had anything to eat?" He was incredulous. No wonder she was so shaky and pale.

"Not today. I just told you that." She snapped at him.

"When was the last time that you had a meal?" he demanded, not the least put off by her show of temper.

"None of your business!" she shouted.

"Are you trying to fucking starve yourself?" He dressed her down like an out of line private.

"Ha! See...I knew you could cuss, if you weren't trying to be so disgustingly polite to impress my grandmother."

"What are you children quarreling about?" Joan demanded.

"I'm hungry. Can we go now?"

"Casey, have you been skipping meals again?" Her hands on her hips, Joan assessed her granddaughter with knowing eyes.

"No." She declared, emphatically, at the same instant that he replied, "Yes."

She glared into his frowning face and then went to the cupboard to find more ibuprofen tablets, downing two and tossing a couple of more in her small, white bag.

JD escorted Gram to the car, and she entered the Italian restaurant on his arm. Casey walked behind the pair. Gram really seemed to enjoy herself, and it was obvious she was getting a kick out of parading around on JD's arm. Heck, why not? Casey figured it had probably been a long time since Gram had such a good looking man, one who wasn't gray, pay so much attention to her.

As for the other ogling females, Casey thought that they should get a load of him in his dress blues. That sight would have folks running for the defibrillators to restore the victims' regular heartbeats. Casey decided she was in the safest spot, behind him and temporarily out of range of his piercing blue eyes. The small parade, led by the hostess, ended at a secluded corner table, which suited Casey just fine. While JD was occupied seating Gram as if he were the reincarnation of Sir Galahad, Casey positioned herself in the corner and tried to fade into the shadows of the dimly lit room.

She wished she was able to relax and enjoy the evening, but she did not trust him. She was losing the daylong battle to subdue the tormenting ache behind her eyes as well as persistent nausea. Her order of minestrone soup and salad set both of her dinner companions on her case. Nibbling on a breadstick and sipping a warm cup of tea, she ignored them and surveyed the coming and going of diners.

Soup was served, and she felt that she had made an excellent choice: it was not disagreeing with her touchy stomach. She focused on her bowl and avoided eye contact as she listened to JD banter with Gram. Still, she could feel his eyes whenever they traveled her way and lingered. Hearing her name, she raised her eyes to meet two familiar faces.

Andy and Alice greeted Casey and her grandmother, who then introduced Jimmy.

Gram insisted that the couple join them. Casey moved over to the vacant chair next to Gram, leaving two unoccupied. Andy, no fool, seated Alice next to Casey, and placed himself between JD and Alice. Casey's sense of humor kicked in at the obvious manipulation.

She was digging into the pocket on her sundress for her vibrating cell while the newcomers placed their order. Casey asked Gram if she wanted to speak with Millie.

"You know that I can't hear on those contraptions. Just ask her what she wants."

"She says that she'll pick you up at nine in the morning."

"Tell her that I will be ready." Gram waved her hand in dismissal.

Casey thought her grandmother's hearing was getting worse. In addition to her lapses in memory, and her occasional bouts of believing Casey was still a child, Gram seemed to get confused and disorientated more lately. It was worrisome to Casey that getting her grandmother to a doctor's office depended on her state of mind and mood when it was time to keep the appointment.

"Millie, she'll be ready, but there is a small snag. Gram has company from out of town. Do you have room for one more on the bus tour? Wonderful! I'll pass on the good news. Oh, don't worry, you'll like him, all the ladies do."

"Okay, Gram you're all set, and you are welcome to bring Jimmy along." A small triumphant laugh escaped before she could squelch it. She didn't look at him as she tucked her phone back into her pocket, but she could feel his blue eyes burning holes through her like two powerful lasers.

"Did you just book him a seat on a senior bus tour?" Alice whispered while covertly glancing at JD.

"Yep. Sure did," she declared, and grinned at him when Alice broke out in a fit of giggles.

Andy spoiled the whole effect by bringing up her plans for tomorrow. "I was surprised to see you here, Casey. I thought Andi told me that you were going to the dispersal? Andy hovered right around six foot and had the same black curls that so frustrated his sister. His dark eyes were always serious, and the direct opposite of his sister's mischievous twinkle in her like colored orbs. Casey always wondered what possessed their mother to call her son Andrew and then name her daughter Andrea. Both were called Andy. They all grew up together and it sometimes got confusing when Casey would call for Andi.

"I had some work to clean up. I'm driving down in the morning."

"I suppose that the two of you troublemakers will terrorize every male on the premises."

"Andy, I'm crushed. You know my heart belongs to you. When Alice gets tired of your sorry butt, I'll be waiting in the wings." Casey gave him an evil little grin and winked at him. Excusing herself, she strolled to the restroom with Alice hot on her heels.

Casey took her time, washed her hands, played with her hair, and applied fresh lip-stain while Alice fired a barrage of questions at her.

"Who is he?"

Casey gave her the spiel about JD being a friend of Gram's.

"He's gorgeous, and those intense blue eyes. Wow!"

She decided not to comment on Alice's critique, or mention the fact that he had affected her much the same way the first time that she'd met him.

"Where is he from? What does he do?" she prodded.

"I guess he is originally from Colorado, but he is in the Marine Corps and is stationed east somewhere. Now can we drop the subject?"

"Sure. Only explain to me why he keeps looking at you like you're dessert?"

"Alice, you're letting your imagination run amok. There's nothing between JD and me, nor will there ever be."

Evidently, JD and Gram had ordered dessert while Casey was playing twenty questions with Alice. A slice of cheesecake was plunked in front of her before she finished her salad. Casey whispered to Alice, "dessert," when cheesecake was served to Gram and apple cobbler à la mode was placed in front of JD. Andy's girlfriend went into another fit of giggles that earned Casey a round of scowls. She did serious damage to the cheesecake and shrugged off Gram's disapproving scowl.

******

Stupid, naive, gullible, take your pick; better yet, she thought, all applied to her. JD had picked up the tab for the meal and he'd been pleasant company for Gram. She did the only hospitable thing and offered to drop him off wherever he was staying before she returned home. Then Gram piped up and told her, "Jimmy is staying with us. He can use the spare room."

The man was smooth, and a lot sneakier than she'd thought.

Men didn't hold car doors open anymore, at least none that she could remember. That sort of courtesy and good manners were expected of the men of Gram's generation. A master manipulator, like him, would know how to exploit those expectations. Now, she was stuck with him as well as a throbbing left cheek. Hell would freeze over before she got into the vehicle without her keys back in her possession.

Why was everything becoming such a hassle? A simple trip to her studio to retrieve a fax had turned into a battle of wills. She even asked politely that he return her keys. He'd turned those penetrating blue eyes on her and asked if she was going out again.

"Not that it is any of your business, Jimmy, but I have to pick up something at my studio." Irked beyond reason and in self-preservation, she spat venom his way. Every demand and unreasonable expectation Mark had piled on her for nearly two years came flooding back. She was not giving JD the opportunity to manipulate her as he'd done to Gram.

"I'll ride along with you. It's late to be going there alone." JD was worried about her frame of mind as well as her safety.

"If I need a bodyguard, I'll hire one. I often return to work much later than this." God, it was only ten thirty! She hadn't had a curfew since high school.

"Well, you shouldn't, and you don't have to tonight. Take Jimmy with you," Gram ordered her with the same commanding voice that she had used with her as a child. It didn't have the desired effect.

"No!" Her siding with JD was the last straw. Twenty years of hurt and betrayal brought out a defiant and cold voice that she'd never turned on Gram. In fact, she realized this new hostility was a recent aberration. It was the same hostile attitude that she'd turned on Mark, the one she turned on Big Joe, and then developed to an art with Susan and attorney Bob Jackson. She was becoming a royal bitch, but it beat being used as a doormat. Gram hauled off and slapped her face as if she still believed her to be a disobedient teen.

"Don't use that tone with me, Casey. Behave and take Jimmy with you."

Casey stuck her chin out and spread her feet wide, facing her grandmother.

"Hell, no!" Gram slapped her again.

"No!" Slap.

"You take him with you, or stay home." Gram issued the ultimatum.

Casey was waiting for the old "you're grounded" to surface from her childhood. She was frustrated with her grandmother's stance and threatened, "I can stay with Andi and check into my own apartment on Monday if I'm no longer welcome here."

"This is your home, but I don't have to put up with your bad attitude or your disrespect. Take Jimmy with you."

Casey stormed out the side door, issuing a more colorful cuss word with every step. She knew her grandmother had issues remembering that Casey was an adult, but this assault was something new in her behavior. JD followed her out the door, but he made sure to keep out of her reach.

She was standing at the driver's side with her hand outstretched. "Keys," she demanded.

"Why don't you let me drive until you calm down?" His calm, reasonable voice set her teeth on edge and stoked her volatile temper.

"Give me the damn keys, Jimmy, or I'll go get my spare set. Do you want to aggravate my grandmother even more?"

"Look, Cassie, be reasonable. You're not in a frame of mind to be driving. Tell me where to go and I will take you there."

She was quick! Skirting him, she made the side door and tried to open it. She pounded several times and cussed a blue streak that would have challenged the vocabulary of some of his troops! Once he realized what she was up to, he sprang into action. JD caught her arm on the backswing and clamped his left hand around her tiny wrist. He pried her fingers from the rock she'd chosen from the edge of a nearby flowerbed with his free hand. She'd been about to heave it through the window on the door. He replaced the rock in her hand with the sought-after keys, but held on to her other arm until she unlocked the passenger side door.

Casey had barely regained her independence from a smothering relationship and was being threatened with another one. She ignored JD on the short trip over to her studio, but he was right on her heels when she unlocked the door and flicked on the lights. She picked up the fax from the bank and placed it into an envelope.

He was wandering the confines of her studio looking at prints of her work and framed awards of recognition that decorated the walls near the small oak conference table that she'd found at a garage sale. She wondered what he thought of her work and why it mattered. "Are you ready to go? I have an early start in the morning, and Millie is picking you and Gram up at nine."

"You think you're really clever, don't you?"

She ignored his sarcastic remark, headed for the door, and held it open. He brushed against her as he exited the open door, ducking to clear the top of the doorframe. A shock went through her at that fleeting touch! I must be losing my mind, she thought. His touch felt like an electrical charge surging through her! Casey shook off the physical effect, turned out the lights, and locked up once more.

As she pulled on to Lorain road, Casey thought that she saw Mark's BMW pull out of the bowling alley across the street, but the dark blue Beamer turned west. She glanced in her mirror a couple of times to make sure he hadn't turned around to follow them east toward the Clague Road intersection. No sign of the car. She figured it was probably someone else. She'd thought she was being covert, but JD picked up on her glances in the rearview or side mirror. "Has he been following you Cassie?"

"Who?"

"Your ex, the one you threatened with the police."

"I'm tired. I probably imagined it."

He decided to put off their conversation until tomorrow. She was beat and in a foul mood.

******

Quiet as a mouse, Casey dressed in a raggedy pair of jeans that contrasted with her new belt and monogrammed buckle. The blue striped shirt, denim jacket, and the horse-embroidered ball cap, purchased in Denver, completed her look for the day. She stuffed the bank letter of credit into the large front right pocket of her jacket and placed her checkbook along with her wallet in the back pockets of her jeans. She tiptoed down the stairs in the predawn darkness carrying her boots. It wouldn't do to wake up the others at this time of the morning.

"Good mornin'."

He almost gave her a heart attack! He was seated at the kitchen table when she rounded the corner on her way to the side entrance. Instinctively, she threw a boot in his direction before she recognized him. He didn't grunt or cuss, so she assumed that she must have missed. "What the hell are you doing in here at this hour?"

"Waiting for you."

"Why?"

"I heard you moving around upstairs and figured it was only a matter of minutes before you tried to sneak out."

"I wasn't sneaking, only attempting to be considerate of people still sleeping."

JD stood, walked close, and handed back the boot that had just clocked him in the shoulder. Casey sat down pulled on her boots and let out a disgusted sigh.

"You and Gram were both aware that I was leaving this morning." She didn't look back, but marched down the three steps to the landing and out the side entrance, punching the garage opener on her way out. He followed her toward the garage.

"What do you think you're doing?"

"Going with you."

"You aren't invited, Jimmy!"

"Look, Cassie, I didn't want to drop in unexpectedly, but you took away my options. All you had to do was return a phone call or an e-mail."

"Move out of the way. I should be on the Interstate by now."

He shook his head and continued to stand behind the Yukon. "You're going to have to run me down to leave without me."

"Don't tempt me."

JD knew she didn't want him around or to discuss the ranch partnership, but she opened the passenger door. She held it open until he got seated, then closed it so hard it shook the vehicle. This is going to be a long miserable day for both of us, he thought. She slipped in a Josh Turner CD and roared down the highway like it was the Daytona 500.

She ignored him completely until she asked, "Do you want to stop for breakfast?"

Still, she didn't look at him, but continued to focus on the highway, and for that he was grateful. "Sounds like a great idea!"

Casey knew he hadn't had breakfast. She pulled into the parking lot and called Andi. "Hi. How's it going?"

"Where are you, Casey?"

"In the parking lot of Bob Evens at seventy-one and three-fifteen. We stopped for breakfast."

"Who're we?"

"An old friend of Gram's from Colorado who decided to tag along."

"Get a booth or table large enough for four. Bonnie and I will be right up."

Casey frowned and disconnected. Without a word, she exited the vehicle. Of course, he was right beside her when she hit the remote lock and stuffed the keys into the front pocket of her jeans.

There was a short wait. Casey made use of the ladies' room, and when she returned, JD was stationed at the entrance. It was as if he expected her to attempt an escape and leave him stranded there. They were seated and had their drinks by the time Andi and Bonnie arrived. Casey made introductions.

Andi was incredulous. "JD is your grandmother's old friend?"

"That's right. You better make your order." Casey nodded toward the waitress who'd just taken Bonnie's order and was waiting for Andi. JD didn't seem to notice the interested stares of Bonnie, Andi, the waitress, and a number of female customers. She wondered if he was really oblivious or only so used to the female attention that it didn't bother him. She decided to change the focus of her two friends. "Did you get in early enough to scout out the sale horses?"

"Bonnie found a couple of yearlings that looked promising."

"No older horses?"

It was Andi who answered the question. Bonnie was preoccupied flirting with JD, and plying him with questions of her own. Bonnie could occupy him for the rest of the day as far as Casey was concerned. Bonnie would buy her time to look over some horses before he could spoil her whole day. "Bonnie figures the broke horses will go for more money. There are several three-in-one packages in the sale catalog."

"What time are they working the broke horses?

"Originally, they had that scheduled for eight, but put it off until nine to accommodate more potential buyers who had called in to say they were stuck in road construction backups."

"I guess that gives us plenty of time to finish our meal." Casey thumbed through the catalog that Andi had brought along.

******

This was working like a charm, Casey thought. Bonnie latched onto JD as soon as they arrived at the farm, and was hauling him around, introducing him to her many friends and associates. Casey and Andi wandered the sale barns, making notes in their catalogs.

At nine o'clock the two friends joined the growing crowd of buyers and spectators lining the perimeter of the large outdoor arena. Several two- and three-year-olds were put through their paces before the older horses began to show their stuff. Casey made a note next to hip number 235, a pretty sorrel mare. "She really looks smooth and is only ten years old."

"I don't know, Casey. She will probably go for a lot of money. She is an AQHA youth champion with several Register of Merits."

The next horse she took note of was a good-looking bay gelding with a star and two hind socks. He was a six-year-old reining horse being offered as a youth or rookie horse, and he really enjoyed his work. The closeness of the crowd didn't seem to faze him, but it was obvious by his profuse sweating that he had been worked down beforehand. She jotted down his hip number 304.

Consigned broodmares started off the catalog. They were followed by farm dispersal mares, which included bred mares, open mares with foals, and three-in-one packages. Their numbers were listed as single and double digits. These were followed by the yearlings and unbroken two-year-olds with numbers in the 100s. Stallions followed, and were also listed in the one hundred grouping.

"It looks like the performance mares and geldings aren't going until late afternoon. Let's find a cool drink, Andi."

Iced tea and a couple of brownies in hand, Casey found a seat at one of the picnic tables set up under the porch-like overhang of the viewing room that had been converted into a combined office and food station. Andi was picking up her number so she could bid on tack that followed the horse auction and hadn't joined her yet. Casey was absorbed in following her notes and didn't notice Duncan approaching. "Casey! As I live and breathe."

She jumped up and gave her old friend a bear hug. "Duncan, how are you?"

"Things are a little rough right now. I've consigned a couple of horses to the sale, but what are you doing here?"

"Looking for a horse."

"For yourself?"

She nodded while chewing on a brownie. Duncan took her catalog and scanned her notes. He pointed to the insert of outside consigned horses and checked five on the list. All were listed under Triple S Performance Horses. "Let me show them to you. I think there are a couple that you might like."

Andi arrived at the table as Casey exited arm in arm with a tall, lanky cowboy that made her mouth water. "Where the heck does she find these guys?"

"What guys?" Bonnie arrived with JD to join them for a lunch break and caught Andi mumbling to herself.

JD was scouting the area looking for Casey. "I thought Casey was with you, Andi?"

"Well… she was, but I got delayed signing up for my auction number, and when I got out here she was wandering over to the stall area with a yummy-looking cowboy." Andi rolled her eyes and exaggerated a sigh while she took note of JD's tightened jaw.

He finished his sandwich and coffee while he talked with Andi, much the same as he'd been doing for hours with Bonnie. He was on a mission to fill in some of the years he'd missed in Cassandra Hoffman's life. She may not want to talk to him, but her friends were more than willing to discuss some of their memories.

Casey was stepping down from a buckskin gelding when he located her, and she continued to totally ignore him. "The gray was fancier and a nice ride, but I really like this one, Duncan." She tried not to groan when JD, Bonnie, and Andi showed up. Casey made introductions and told Bonnie, "You should look at the two yearlings and the three-year-old mare that Duncan brought to the sale, if you haven't already seen them."

She walked the buckskin back to his stall while Bonnie was looking at the other horses. JD followed, but kept his distance. Casey headed for the bleachers. She turned to him. "JD, would you get me a bottle of water? I need to make a pit stop before we find our seats."

******

Bonnie's trailer was full. She'd purchased Duncan's three-year-old mare, one of his yearling geldings, and the gray that Casey rode before the buckskin that she now owned. Bonnie also bought a tall, leggy yearling that she thought would have the potential for a hunter.

Casey made arrangements with Duncan to drop her new horse off at Bonnie's place on his way back to Pennsylvania.

Casey was beat, so they left before the tack auction. She relinquished the driving chore to JD. "Do you want to stop for dinner, Cassie?"

"Let me check with Gram first." It took her grandmother a long time to answer. "Hi Gram. Did I wake you?... Have you eaten dinner?... Okay, Jimmy and I'll stop on the way home. Can we bring you anything?" After her brief conversation with her grandmother, she informed JD, "Gram and Millie had dinner after the bus tour."

"Where do you want to go?"

"Exit at Route 82. There are plenty of places to choose from."

They ended up at a seafood restaurant.

Casey sighed, "It was so sad, the prices those beautiful horses sold for. I wish I could have bought more of them."

"You could have."

"No, I couldn't, and even if I could afford to buy them, I couldn't board more than one."

"You have a ranch in Colorado where you could keep them."

"Don't spoil my appetite with this ranch crap."

"Okay, what do you want to talk about?"

The devil got the better of her. "How about you and Bonnie?"

His eyes took on a mischievous glint. "Nothing to tell."

"Yeah, right! So, how about you tell me about my father instead?"

"I hung around doing chores when he came back home. He was really messed up, both physically and mentally. Hindsight, he was probably suffering major trauma and had PTSD. I've seen a lot of that since, but at the time I didn't recognize it. I kept up the place while he was in and out of the hospital and rehab. I guess that's where he met Susan; her first husband was in the same semi-private room. I kept hoping he would bring you home. He shared the photos and letters from your grandmother with me up until you were age ten. Then one day I returned on spring break and he was gone. He had left an envelope for me with some money and instructions to keep the ranch in good repair for your return. He talked about you all the time, and the photos as well as the letters were well worn from handling."

"Did he ever tell you why he abandoned me?"

Her voice cracked, and he could tell she was willing the tears filling her eyes not to fall. "I didn't know until recently that he had. Bill would come back with stories of how well you were doing. I saw a video of your first dance recital, first walk trot riding class, and I assumed that he'd taken them while visiting with you."

"Gram probably took videos and forward them the same as she did with the letters and photos, through Bob Jackson."

"Did Bob tell you that?"

"No. He made a lot of excuses for my father's absence in my life. He also used the fact I resembled my mother to a degree that was too painful for my father to get a grip on it."

"You didn't think he was telling the truth?"

"He was hiding something. There is more to this than my uncanny resemblance to my mother."

"Maybe Bob could have shared more with you if you'd stayed put."

"I'd had enough of him, as well as his manipulations and excuses for my father. He could've come clean after you and Big Joe left the night we had dinner. Instead, he kept dropping breadcrumbs, trying to lure me in." Casey pushed aside her half-eaten cheese cake, "And I've had too much to eat and more than enough of this topic. I really need some sleep. Duncan is delivering Bucky early in the morning, and I want to be there."

JD dropped the conversation and paid the check.

******

Time was running out. He was booked on a flight to the East Coast on Monday morning, and tomorrow was his last full day. A lot was left unsaid and unsettled, but he didn't want to push her. If he did, she would most likely sever all ties with him as she had with Bob. However, he fully intended to tag along to the boarding stable, even if it meant dodging Bonnie again. *I'm sure not letting her meet Duncan alone*, he thought. Cassie might have been oblivious to the heated looks the other man cast her way, but he sure wasn't.

Prior to Cassie reentering his life, JD would've most likely taken Bonnie up on her blatant sexual advances, but he hadn't been interested in other women since being reunited with Cassandra Hoffman back in Denver. He was becoming possessive about her, even though she'd made it clear that she didn't want anything to do with him. If he couldn't work out the business of the ranch partnership with her, how was he going to keep in touch?

Chapter 6

JD sat on the front stoop of Joan Curtis' little house, enjoying the soft summer rain. He was also looking back over the last few days with Cassie and lost opportunities to get closer to her. He'd spent a large part of the afternoon at the barn with her, helping move her tack into the assigned locker that matched Bucky's stall number. Once her new horse was settled, they returned home to escort her grandmother to church. He offered to take them out for dinner, but Cassie refused to go unless she paid for the meal. She was making him crazy! She wasn't interested in the money that her father had left her, nor did she want anything to do with the ranch.

It was raining harder now. This is sure a different world from the one I grew up in, he thought, or the stinking desert where I will soon be deployed. My third tour of Iraq facing me, and I hate the place more with each return. Even when I'm not in the war-zone it stays with me. I can't sit on a step in the rain on a quiet dead end street without feeling that someone is lurking in the dark corners where the streetlights don't reach.

More and more of his sleep was disrupted by haunting images of white hot heat radiating off the desert sand and pockmarked white buildings. Eyes tracked his unit's progress as they patrolled the streets and alleyways. Were they the wary eyes of the innocent inhabitants frightened out of their wits, or were they the intent stares of insurgent snipers?

He gave himself a mental shake, but still couldn't escape the feeling that he was being observed. All thoughts fled when Cassie stepped out the door behind him.

******

Rain beating on the roof woke Casey with an urgent need to relieve her bladder. The change in the weather had her head feeling like a balloon ready to burst, so she checked for her stash of ibuprofen. "Oh, crap!" She was all out of her supply and grumbled, "I guess I'll have to try downstairs. Maybe Gram has a store of aspirin in the first floor bath medicine cabinet."

She worked her way down to the main floor without turning on the lights. The nightlights in the hall, bathroom, and kitchen helped her navigate. With pills on their way into her system targeting her throbbing sinuses, she refilled her glass from the water dispenser on the fridge. She noticed the open front door on her way back to her room. *Jeez, Gram you are really slipping!* She was thinking that her grandmother's decline could be worse than she thought, and was trying to figure out how to get her belligerent fanny to the doctor for a checkup.

Casey saw him shirtless and barefoot sitting on the front stoop as she was about to close and lock up. Instead, she opened the screen door and sat on the step beside him. "What are you doing out here?"

"Enjoying the rain."

Something was bothering him, and she figured he was unable to sleep. "Well…it's a good thing it's the middle of the night. Otherwise 911 would be overrun with calls from women on this end of Frank Street complaining of heart palpitations."

"What about you? That T-shirt barely reaches mid-thigh! Do you run around out here dressed like that often?"

She wanted to smack him. It was his fault she was out here in her nightshirt. Casey decided to change the subject. "You're not doing it right."

"Doing what right."

"The whole rain thing!"

He'd no idea what she was talking about and was about to ask for clarification when she set her water glass on the stoop, walked onto the lawn, and began twirling in the rain. This wasn't the little girl performing at a dance recital, but a pagan goddess who could be a serious contender in a wet T-shirt contest!

Casey held out her arms to him. "Come on, Jimmy boy, haven't you ever danced in the rain?"

He was finding it hard to control his physical response to her erotic rain dance. "Can't say that I ever have."

She walked up and took hold of his hands, "Well, it's about time you gave it a try!"

A very short time later, the thought occurred to her, maybe she should have left him on the front porch. What started out as a couple dancing a simple two-step quickly turned into a carnal embrace.

JD lifted Casey off her feet and kissed her. God, he'd wanted to hold her and kiss her ever since he had seen her in Denver, but this unexpected encounter was getting out of hand! All reasonable thought left him when she put her arms around his neck and instigated a tongue-thrusting kiss.

Casey's female core responded to him like it had never done to anyone before. She couldn't get close enough to him. When he cupped her butt urging her close to his erection, she opened her legs to wrap them around him.

"What are you children doing out in the pouring rain?"

Oh God! It was Gram! Casey disengaged her grip on JD the instant he took his hands off her, and she went tumbling to the soggy lawn in a fit of laughter.

"Casey, stop acting like a crazy person before the neighbors call the police! Come in the side door; I don't want you kids tracking up my living room carpet."

Kids? Oh boy, here we go again, she thought. "I hope she doesn't forget to open the side door. She just closed and locked this one."

JD didn't say a word, but waited for her to pick up her glass. Then he took her arm as they crossed the lawn and worked their way up the drive to the now unlocked entrance.

Gram was waiting for them on the landing of the side entry. "Go down and towel off, while I make you some hot chocolate. I ought to take a switch to both of you. You'll be lucky if you don't come down with pneumonia!"

Casey flicked on the basement light and went straight to the dryer to pull out a couple of fresh towels. Armed with a clean shirt and a pair of boxer shorts, she changed in the small gray tiled bathroom.

"I'll run up and get you a clean pair of britches. Use the shower if you want. I'll be right back."

His dress uniform was hung in the closet of the guest room, but everything he had worn in the past few days was stuffed into a large plastic bag inside his duffel. She pulled out the dirty laundry and located a clean pair of briefs as well as a pair of jeans. She carried it all down stairs receiving a quelling look of disapproval as she passed her grandmother. Casey knocked on the bathroom door, "Throw out the wet trousers and I'll give you the dry ones." He threw out the wet jeans and took the dry offerings. She picked up the wet jeans. "Is that it?"

"Yeah. Unless you want the towels too."

"No. I'll get them later with the rest of the linens." Lord, she thought, he didn't have any underwear on, and neither did I! If it hadn't been for Gram's timely interruption I could be in a world of hurt. She'd be willing to bet he didn't have a condom handy. She surely hadn't, nor had the use of birth control even entered her mind. She threw his mixed load of laundry into the washer and set the temperature selector to cold. She trudged up the stairs like a kid who'd been caught with her hand in a cookie jar, and JD was right behind her.

Gram plunked a mug of hot chocolate, complete with mini marshmallows, in front of each on them. Dressed in a pink flannel nightgown and matching quilted robe, she sat down at the table with her own mug and lowered the boom. "I'm really disappointed in both of you. My granddaughter cavorting in the rain like some kind of demented wood nymph! As for you, young man, you have almost a decade on her and should know better."

"Yes, Ma'am. Sorry Ma'am, it won't happen again."

Casey lost it and broke into another fit of laughter. Gram got up and smacked her! That reprimand only made her laugh harder. Smack! At that point JD protested, "Honestly, Mrs. Curtis, the whole thing was as much my fault as Cassie's."

"See! So why don't you go smack Jimmy in the chops?"

"Because he apologized for his inappropriate behavior, you naughty girl, and I don't doubt for an instant that you instigated the whole episode."

What could she say? She really did start the fireworks with her silly rain dance. The washer completed its cycle and saved her any more verbal abuse. She folded the rest of the towels and other personal items that were in the dryer before putting JD's things in.

She could hear them in deep conversation though she couldn't make out the words over the mechanical workings of the dryer. She curled up in her grandpa's old recliner that had long ago been relegated to the bowels of the house Casey pulled a faded green lap robe from the back of the like colored La-Z-Boy to ward off the chills wracking her body.

A short while later, Casey watched JD descend the stairs with a mug in each hand, and she covertly wiped her tears with the ancient afghan. He offered her one of the mugs and pulled out an old armchair that matched the recliner. JD positioned it so he would be facing her.

"What are you doing down here, Cassie?"

She sipped the hot chocolate before answering. "I'm waiting for the dryer to stop. I imagine you will want to pack your clean clothing before you leave this morning."

"You did my laundry?" He sounded astonished.

"Why does that shock you? I'm quite capable of performing the daily humdrum of domestic chores."

"I didn't mean it that way. It's only that I've been doing it for myself for a longtime. Thank you."

"We really don't know much about each other. However, you probably know more about me, thanks to Bob Jackson."

"What do you want to know?"

"Start with your father driving Gram and me home. I don't recall much at all."

"Pop offered to make the trip to bring you here. I rode along."

"Didn't that pull you out of school?'

"At the time, everyone thought that it was better that I made the trip to help you transition, and to keep Pop company on the return trip."

"Well…why the heck all the animosity floating around the dinner table in Denver? It wasn't all my doing."

"Joe is still trying to have our father declared incompetent to nullify his will. He's also bent on tagging me as someone else's bastard."

"What a creep! What does your mother have to say about it?"

"My mother died in childbirth when I was quite young."

"I'm sorry JD. Gram never told me your mother was gone too."

He wanted to know about her, not rehash his dysfunctional family. "Did your grandmother hit you a lot when you were a kid?"

"No. I got plenty of tongue-lashings, though. I think she's smacked me more the last couple of days than in my entire life! Her doctor thinks she has the onset of Alzheimer's, and it sometimes results in aggressive behavior. Stop changing the subject; finish telling me about you. Did your mom's baby survive?"

"No. My baby sister lost her life too."

"Sorry, but you were telling me about your nemesis."

"Big Joe was really in a rage when our father sold Bill Hoffman part of the ranch. Pop Jim set up your ranch as a bumper between what's Big Joe's ranch and what now belongs to me. The largest underground water reservoir in the immediate area is located on the place my pop sold to your father. The proceeds from the sale to Bill went into a trust for Pop's grandkids. Joe went to court to contest the will. He managed to get his hands on my DNA and claims to have proof of paternity filed with the court."

"Can't you fight that?"

"Pop Jim wasn't anyone's fool. He deposited with Bob Jackson an earlier paternity test that proved him as my father. He knew Joe too well and must've had a premonition of things to come. Joe's best hope now is that I don't make it back from my next deployment."

"Wow! Then my father left his ranch to you and me. That really had to piss him off."

"That's a huge understatement. He tried to buy the place from Bill, but the best he could negotiate was a thirty-year lease, but you probably already know that. Your dad was busy working on water conservation projects at the University of Kansas, in those days, and he didn't have the time or inclination to run the ranch, but he wasn't selling. He'd bought it to raise his young family. With Bill's passing, Big Joe sees a new opportunity to obtain the ranch"

The dryer timer buzzed. Casey polished off her hot chocolate and went to unload the machine. Together they folded his clean clothing while she processed this new information. His military style of folding was a far cry from her haphazard style that received constant criticism from Gram.

Dawn was breaking when they once more traversed the small kitchen to the hall leading to the bedrooms.

"What time is your flight?"

"Nine-forty."

"I'll change my clothes and drive you to the airport. After you check in, we can find some breakfast while we wait for your flight."

******

Casey drove to the stable, and took Bucky on a long ride in the park. All the replays of the past few days, the time spent in Denver, and the sense of loss that she'd experienced as JD passed through the security gate to board his flight crowded her mind.

There wasn't much point in even attempting to work. It always cleared her thoughts and soothed her inner turmoil to ride a good horse. Her new buckskin was a really good horse. They hit it off immediately, and he seemed to enjoy the trails as much as she did.

Gram had dinner on by the time Casey got home. She took a quick shower before joining her grandmother at the table. Gram appeared better today, more like her old self.

"Jimmy is gone. He left me a note thanking me for my hospitality."

"Yeah, I knew he was gone. I drove him to the airport this morning."

"Do you think he will visit us again?"

"I don't know, Gram." Casey was having a hard time swallowing and keeping the tears from forming. She set her fork on her plate before continuing. "He is on his way to Iraq or somewhere, Gram. God knows when we'll see him again." An unbidden thought flitted through her mind: or even if I'll ever see him again. The persistent tears spilled over at the very thought of never seeing him again.

Chapter 7

Big Joe bellowed into the phone, "What the hell do you mean he spent the weekend with her?"

"I got some really interesting footage."

"Not over the phone! Meet me in Denver for lunch. You know the place."

Big Joe downed the drink he'd just poured then pitched the expensive crystal decanter of the amber liquid across the office. "That son of a bi——" His tirade was interrupted as his son Spencer burst through the door.

"What the hell is the matter with you? It sounded like a damn bomb went off in here." Spencer had a feeling that JD had something to do with Big Joe's foul mood.

"Find Harrison. You and your brother will have to run this operation for a few days. I have some business to take care of in Denver."

******

Stokes was already at the bar when Big Joe arrived. The PI was a smidgen under six foot, and not very impressive. That fact and his patient persistent nature served him well and enabled him to blend in almost anywhere. His light brown receding hairline and brown eyes framed by wire-rimmed glasses didn't garner much interest.

An overly attentive young hostess escorted Big Joe to his usual table at the back corner of the dining room where he had an excellent view of who came and went. He had more than a few enemies. That was to be expected. He was a rich, ruthless, powerful man who was about to move JD to the top of his enemy list.

He ordered another bourbon when Stokes joined him and waved off the waiter as he returned for their lunch order. "Get on with it."

Stokes disliked Big Joe, but he paid well and had a lot of well-heeled connections. Things were tight, so he took on the assignment to follow Cassandra Hoffman. "Not much happened after she got back from Denver. She works at her studio and spends a lot of time at home with her grandmother. Other than a couple of altercations with her ex fiancé, not much to interest you until JD showed up, but it is all in the report."

Big Joe took the packet with the report, complete with photos, and set it aside. He would review it in private. "Get to the part about JD."

"He must have arrived by cab. I didn't know he was there, but stuck around a while when she got home. It was obvious that something was out of the ordinary that Friday evening. She broke the speed limit and then some. A short time later she, her grandmother, and JD went out to eat. He stayed the night, but before dawn they were on the road. I followed them with the little tracking beacon I'd placed on her vehicle when I'd first taken on the assignment. They spent the day at a horse sale with some of her friends. Early Sunday morning, the pair of them went to a local boarding stable where her purchase of the prior day was delivered. They returned home to escort her grandmother to church."

Stokes placed a flash drive in his laptop and activated the file he wanted then he slid it over for Big Joe to view. "Sunday, the lights went out around eleven. I stayed for a while and figured they were in for the night. It was raining, and I was ready to pack it up when JD opened the door and seated himself on the small covered porch. Things got interesting when Miss Hoffman joined him."

Big Joe closed the laptop. "Stokes, I want that flash drive."

Stokes ejected it and gave it to his client who dropped it into the packet with the rest the results from his assignment.

"Go back and keep an eye on her. I will take care of JD."

Stokes didn't like the sounds of the implied threat, but he caught the next flight back to Cleveland.

******

A nice quiet supper at home was exactly what the doctor had ordered for Gram, and Casey thought it was a welcome relief for her, too. Her life had been in a constant turmoil for past couple of months, and she hadn't kept a close eye on the continuing decline of her grandmother.

Millie was a godsend. In addition to being Gram's best friend, she was a dependable resource for Casey when she had to be away for part of the day. Casey enjoyed Millie's visits as much as her grandmother did. Gram's friend was a bubbly, happy person who was well traveled and well spoken. She was an entertaining as well as brilliant conversationalist.

Millie checked in a tad shorter than Gram, who was only five feet six inches tall, as was Casey. Millie's white hair always looked like she had just stepped out of a beauty salon, and her brown eyes always twinkled. A few extra pounds had found their way onto her delicate frame, but she was still a striking woman at seventy-eight. She was Gram's social link to the to the rest of the world. In addition to their regular senior activities, they went to movies and dinner several times a month. They shopped together, and Millie often shared lunch or dinner with them in Gram's kitchen.

The lease was up on the studio at the end of September, and Casey was considering setting up her desktop computer and filing cabinets in the spare bedroom. The conversion of the room would be easy to accomplish. It would substantially reduce her phone charges at the leased studio, as well as the monthly rent and insurance on the place. Easels and painting supplies could occupy a spot in the basement along with the conference table. She could meet with prospective clients in a room at the library. Working out of the house would allow her to be home more, should Gram need her.

August rolled around, and Casey was sure she was being followed. She mentioned the stalker to Bonnie while hosing off Bucky.

"Have you notified the police?"

"No. At first I thought it was Mark following me. I threatened him with jail time for stalking, and he backed off. Word is that he's fixated on someone else now. It was the BMW in the bowling alley on the opposite side of the street from the studio, the night JD came to town, that made me think it was Mark."

"Do you know who it is?"

"I don't have a clue. The cars have changed a few times, but from what fleeting glimpses I get, it is always the same person."

"I'll check with my cousin Chuck. He is on the NOPD and might know the best way to proceed. If he's been following you around for several months, that is downright creepy."

Casey paid closer attention to what she determined was a stalker and was able to give a better description to Detective Chuck Bennett. She filed an official complaint, and within a week the police apprehended the man.

Hiram Stokes refused to talk other than to say he was a PI and working for a client when he was arrested on the stalking charge. He immediately requested a lawyer, and then clammed up.

"I don't know, Casey, he won't say a word. I mentioned that he was not a licensed PI in the state of Ohio, nor did he contact local law enforcement or register within this state." Detective Chuck Bennett was updating Casey.

"Where is he licensed?"

"His license was issued in Colorado. He seems more worried about giving up his client than spending time locked up."

"Well, Chuck, if he's working for Big Joe Gannon, he will have a longer, healthier life in the slammer than going against his client."

"Why would this Gannon guy be keeping tabs on you?"

"I don't know, but I'll make a couple of phone calls and be back to you in a day or so. Are you able to hold him that long?"

"Oh, yeah. His rental car and hotel room were chuck full of photos, videos, and notebooks on you; we can hold him until the arraignment. There is a substantial backlog, so we have a few days to build our case and for you to press charges."

Casey didn't wait to leave the parking lot of the police station before placing a phone call to Bob Jackson. While she waited for the call to be routed to him, she mulled over her best approach.

"Casey, what a pleasant surprise! How can I help you?"

"You may not think this is so pleasant when I inform you that I've had your private investigator arrested." She paused for effect, "His name is Hiram Stokes, and he's licensed in Colorado. Ring any bells?"

"I will have my people check him out, but he wasn't hired by this law firm."

"Well…assuming you are being truthful, I think the suspects narrow down to either Big Joe or JD."

"JD wouldn't pay to have you followed. I thought things were straightened out between the two of you?"

"What would make you think that?"

"He came to see me after visiting with you, and changed his will."

"I haven't heard from him since he boarded his flight out of here. However, I'm inclined to eliminate him. The first time I noticed Mr. Stokes, JD was with me and I thought it was my ex who was following us. Stokes put a tracking device on my Yukon. He's not talking to the detectives, so we don't know how long it has been in place."

The following day, Stokes asked to speak to Casey. Detective Bennett and Stokes sat in a small interrogation room, minus his attorney.

"Thank you for agreeing to see me, Ms. Hoffman."

"Get to the point, Mr. Stokes. Did Joe Gannon hire you to follow me?"

Stokes tried hard to swallow, but his spit had dried up at the mention of Big Joe's name. Unable to answer, he merely nodded his head in answer to her question.

"Why?"

"Hypothetically, he may be concerned that JD could sway you over to his side in the legal battle over the property and assets of the late James Donovan Gannon Sr."

"What else?"

"He was in a rage over the footage that I took of the two of you in the rain the hours preceding your early morning trip to the airport."

"Why would he care about that?"

"I don't know for sure, but it did appear, to him, JD was making inroads with you. I was sent back here to keep tabs on you while he took care of JD."

"What does that mean?"

"It beats me, but there was a definite threat implied."

Had something happened to JD, and that was the reason she'd not heard from him? She had to find out. She reached out to Bob Jackson with her concerns. He had a long-standing relationship with JD. Casey prayed for news of the marine captain with the captivating blue eyes. Her mind was rife with questions: where are you, JD? Why don't you answer my e-mails or letters?

Chapter 8

The earth shook, the building swayed, and glass rained down as the marines gathered dove for cover beneath the mess hall tables. Sergeant Rick O'Bannon grabbed his half-eaten lunch as he took cover. "It seems those suicide loonies always pick mealtime to pursue martyrdom."

"They know we gather here for meals, and it's the best time to inflict maximum casualties if they can breach the outer perimeter."

"Hell, Captain, many more blasts like that and the whole place could crumble around our ears."

JD had to agree with his sergeant on the intensity of the blast, but what worried him more was the frequency of patrols and missions assigned to his men. Lately, they'd been given every dirty or hazardous assignment that came down the pike.

He didn't like or trust the paid military contractors assigned to escort and protect the fat cats looking to profit off the destruction of Iraq. The mercs tended to make the jobs of the troops more difficult, and you sure didn't want them behind your back any more than you did some of the questionable Iraqis. O'Bannon had killed a mercenary who had JD in his cross hairs while they were on patrol the day before. Now, there was an investigation into his sergeant's shooting of a private contractor.

JD figured it was time to resign his commission and try on civilian life. His presence was becoming an added danger to his command. A recent update from Bob had him rethinking his priorities. Retiring from the Marine Corps wasn't any longer a goal; getting home alive was his new focus. He hoped that he lived long enough to put Big Joe six feet under. Bob warned him to watch his back. "All I've been able to find out is that there is a contract on you."

Big Joe's greed and hatred of him evidently knew no bounds. Did he have enough influence to reach out to arrange hazardous missions be assigned? JD knew his adversary had friends in high places and could easily have hired one of the private security people as a hit man. Who would question his death in a war littered with suicide bombers, hostile insurgents, IEDs, and snipers? Other troops killed as a result of Big Joe's vendetta against JD would be acceptable collateral damage.

Neither Bob nor he would have known about the hit out on him if Cassie hadn't called Bob to advise him of the threat. It really galled him that Big Joe was having her followed. JD worried that changing his will to leave her what he owned could have put her in danger.

Well…two can play this game. Captain JD Gannon sent for Sergeant O'Bannon. JD had been attempting to put Cassie in the back of his mind and concentrate on the job at hand. Homesick and love struck fools got themselves and others killed.

******

Casey hadn't heard from JD at all, yet Bob Jackson managed to reach him to pass on the threat that Stokes related to her in August. She sighed as she cubed day-old bread to make stuffing for tomorrow's turkey. Her subconscious kept nagging at her: did his lack of communication mean he wanted to sever their tenuous relationship? Pumpkin and spice filled the air from the cooling pies on the counter. She was experiencing an uncharacteristic lack of enthusiasm for Thanksgiving and the approaching holiday season.

Gram and Millie's arrival helped eliminate Casey's persistent funk. "How was your evening at the movies?"

Gram merely grunted, but Millie laughed, "Joan dozed off several times, missing much of the plot. Oh, and by the way, we picked up a pumpkin roll from the DQ on our trip back here." Millie handed the bag with the roll to Casey.

She brewed a fresh pot of tea and removed the breadcrumbs from the kitchen table. "You are joining us for dinner tomorrow, aren't you, Millie?"

"I'll be here at three with my homemade applesauce, dinner rolls, and a huge appetite."

They shared the dessert, a hot cup of tea, and a few hands of gin rummy.

The Thanksgiving turkey was spectacular, as were the pies! Casey ate way too much and felt like one of the large helium balloons that had floated above the televised parade earlier in the day. Gram and Millie were making plans to join in the shopping madness of the following morning. Casey didn't doubt that the two bargain hunters would be in the throngs, waiting for the doors to open at the box stores on the stroke of midnight if they were a few decades younger.

Gram retired soon after Millie left to rest up for their Christmas shopping binge. The next morning, Casey put on the teakettle and went to check on her grandmother, who she figured must have overslept.

"Gram, Millie will be here in less than an hour." Her grandmother didn't respond. Casey turned on the overhead light and returned to the side of the bed. Gram's eyes were following her. However, Joan Curtis was unable to speak, the left side of her face was sagging, and she was unable to move or grasp her granddaughter's hand. Casey saw the panic in her grandmother's faded blue eyes.

The teakettle began to screech. "I'll be right back, Gram!" Casey turned off the burner and called 911 from the kitchen phone. She unlocked the doors for the paramedics before returning to her grandmother's bedside.

She met Millie in the drive as the paramedics lifted Gram into the ambulance. Gram's friend was distraught. "I'm so sorry, Millie, I should've called you, but it slipped my mind."

"Don't worry about it, dear. I understand. I will meet you at the hospital."

To Casey, the ride over to Fairview Hospital went agonizingly slow. Time was of the essence with a stroke victim, and she didn't have a clue what time of the night Gram had been afflicted. Casey wanted to remain by her grandmother's side as she was rushed through the emergency room, but was waylaid filling out the admitting paperwork and waiting for input and computer verification of Gram's medical history, doctor, and insurance.

For three days, she prayed for a miracle as she held her grandmother's hand. Her prayers changed after the second day from "please don't take her from me" to "don't let her suffer." Casey wasn't sure whether Gram knew she was there. Casey recalled how Gram had been confusing Casey with Kathryn of late. Casey felt a hollow emptiness take possession of her as she witnessed the last of her family pass from this world.

Casey was nonplused, but still grateful that Millie had a copy of Gram's will as well as her prepaid funeral documents. "Why didn't Gram tell me she'd made plans like this?"

"Joan changed her will and prepaid her funeral following her birthday this past May."

"Did she tell you why she wanted to be cremated?"

"She didn't like the idea of decomposing and being worm food."

Casey snorted and laughed for the first time since the day after Thanksgiving. "Worm food?"

"That's what she said. There's a letter that she gave me in July in this packet along with some photos she said you've never seen."

Joan's granddaughter couldn't bring herself to open the envelope until the week after the memorial service. Gram's ashes had been laid to rest next to her husband.

The photos enclosed within the packet were of her family. Mom and Dad holding the small child that she had been, her brothers, and Jimmy Gannon were included in the faded photos. Each photo was handwritten on the reverse side and began with a 1985 date. Bill Jr. and his friend Jimmy were both thirteen, Carson was ten, and of course, she was only five that summer. She carefully put the images of her family back into the large envelope, got up and made a cup of hot tea, and stared at the legal-size envelope with her name on it. She ignored it as she proceeded to the living room to dismantle the Christmas tree that she and Gram had decorated on the Tuesday before Thanksgiving.

It haunted her. Unable to sleep, she opened the envelope. Fortified with a fresh cup of tea— more brandy than tea—she opened the letter bomb.

July 30, 2006
My darling Casey,
I know that you were upset with the lack of follow-up by Jimmy after you left him at the airport. I twisted Bob Jackson's arm to get to the bottom of Jimmy's strange behavior. First let me say that I did not know any of what I am going to tell you, nor do I believe most of it.

Jimmy got a registered letter a few weeks after he left here from someone named Big Joe. He states in the letter that he is your biological father and Jimmy should cease his incestuous relations with you. I can't believe that Kathryn would ever cheat on Bill, and I told Bob that very thing.

Bill was depressed, heavily sedated, and this, Big Joe, person managed to convince him Kathryn had turned to him out of neglect and loneliness. How he was able to accomplish the ruse was something that Bob would not share with me. He did say your father took the accusation to heart. Bob also told me he is your attorney and could answer your questions. It is his belief this person is now using this assertion as a wedge between you and Jimmy.

My mind is not what it was, so I am writing this down before I forget the conversation. Maybe this falsehood was part of the reason your father never came to see you. I always felt it was more than your uncanny resemblance to Kathryn that kept him away.

Sell the house, Casey. Use the money to start a new life. If you are reading this before I can manage to tell you of Big Joe's treachery in person, I no longer need the house, and neither do you.

I leave you my earthly possessions and all my love.

Grandma Joan

Casey reread the letter several times. Her tears gradually washed away the sadness. It was replaced with a deep-seated need for revenge.

Andi agreed to house- and horse-sit while Casey flew to Denver to confront Bob Jackson and Big Joe Gannon.

******

JD's mind was playing tricks on him. The sounds of the blast and resulting screams constantly rolled around in his head for so long that the strange new sound brought on panic. *Christmas music? I remember some of the carols. It didn't make sense, but he was too tired to figure it out.*

JD opened his eyes for the first time in six weeks, and pain flashed through the sockets to his brain. "Turn the damn lights out!" He ordered, but no one heard him. All that came out was a scratchy gagging sound. Once more he attempted to open his eyes, much slower this time. He tried to focus and concentrate on assessing his current situation: a tube was stuck down his throat, oxygen tubes invaded his nasal passages, a catheter had been inserted to drain his bladder, IV needles were taped to his left hand, and leads had been taped to his chest for the machines constantly monitoring his every breath and heartbeat. *Damn, I'm in a fucking hospital. How the hell did I get here, and where is here?*

The inventory was exhausting; the dark void enveloped him before he could sort out the questions plaguing him.

Chapter 9

Casey checked into the Best Western near the airport and called Bob Jackson from there. She kicked her winter boots off and plunked onto the king size bed while she waited for Bob's administrative assistant, Mary, to inform him she was on the line.

"I'm sorry, Miss Hoffman, Mr. Jackson is in a meeting with another client. Would you give me number where he can reach you?"

"He has my cell number." She ended the call, dug the charger out of her handbag, plugged it into the outlet near the oak desk that provided a workspace for business travelers, and sprawled across the bed.

She was sound asleep soon after her head hit the pillow. *"Stop! Don't go. I need to talk to you. Please, tell me why you're haunting me?" But as always, he backed away to retreat behind the same large, ominous shadow.* Casey woke to the musical tones of her phone, but she ignored it. Instead, she reached for the sketchpad and pencil she'd placed on the nightstand near the house phone. She clicked on the brass lamp, swung her legs over the edge of the bed, and began sketching like she was possessed.

It had been eight months, and the same dream persisted. She had found in her research that it was recommended to write down what you could remember of a dream immediately upon waking, while it was fresh. Words failed her, so she sketched what she could before the visions were lost. Her pencil stalled as the figure in her dream faded.

Casey's phone intruded once more. This time she crossed the rust-colored Berber carpet to answer it. The display told her the caller was Bob Jackson. "Hello, Bob."

"Casey, it's good to hear your voice. Do you have an arrival time?"

"I'm already in Denver and checked in at the Best Western on Tower." She crossed the room and reopened the rust, tan, and green striped drapes that matched the now slept-on bedspread.

"Have you had dinner yet?"

"No. I needed a nap more than food."

"I'll pick you up in an hour, and we can have dinner together."

"This is business, Bob, and the last time I had dinner with you was not very productive."

"Look, we both have to eat. And, I promise, not a single interruption this time. Do you like Mexican food?"

"Mexican is fine. Is casual okay where we're going? I'm not in a mood to get all gussied up."

"Casual is fine."

The Tamayo restaurant on Larimer Street had a warm décor that was spectacular with its amber and coral-colored walls, highlighting exquisite artwork that included silver-encrusted toucans, silver and volcanic rock guacamole bowls, and Mayan masks to keep a watchful eye over the patrons. Families as well as business folk occupied the main dining room. She fit right in with her tan plaid shirt, jeans, denim jacket, and boots. Bob was still in his work duds, making them a bit of a mismatch. "Isn't this a bit strange to have a private room all to ourselves, Bob?"

"I thought privacy was in order for our discussion."

Casey followed Bob's lead and ordered the roasted salmon, but refused the margarita, opting for water and a clear head. After ordering, she handed Bob the packet her grandmother had left for her. He took a swig of the margarita placed in front of him, biding time until the server exited. "Your grandmother was correct; your mother would never have cheated on your father."

"Then how can Big Joe claim I'm his daughter?" The roast salmon was delicious, but it went down like hot lead to do battle with the nacho appetizer already keeping time with the mariachi music. Maybe Mexican food hadn't been such a great choice given the dinner subject matter?

"Before you were born, Bill used to occasionally accompany Big Joe on hunting trips and frequent excursions to his favorite bar. Bill related to me later that Big Joe methodically developed social ties with your family. Your mother and brothers were invited to the annual Fourth of July bash at Big Joe's ranch. That's where they first met JD. He was the same age as Bill Jr., and they hit it off."

Casey changed her mind and ordered a rum and Coke, figuring she might need a little fortification. "I can't imagine my parents becoming friendly with the likes of Big Joe."

"In those days, Big Joe was into putting on a friendly face and turning on the charm to get closer to his ultimate goals. In your parents' case, it was getting his hands on the ranch his father had sold to Bill. Kathryn didn't like Big Joe or his dragging Bill along on his drinking binges. A sheriff's deputy escorted them home on the night in question. Big Joe was taken home first. His wife refused him entry to the house, so Bill offered to let him stay for the night." He paused to order another drink. "Big Joe said he impregnated Kathryn that night."

"And my father just took his word for it? What did my mother have to say about it?"

"Big Joe didn't make the claim until after your mother was dead, and Bill had returned home from the hospital." He drained his drink before switching to black coffee. "Big Joe told your dad that he was sleeping on the couch when Kathryn went upstairs to check on Carson, who had a bad cold and was fussing. Big Joe claimed that they got cozy on the couch after she returned to the main floor."

"Wait just a damn minute! You mean my father believed that crap?" She ignored the queasiness and the threat of a recycled dinner.

"At that point, your father was recovering from a traumatic brain injury, in addition to horrid flashbacks of the accident. Bill had already given Big Joe a thirty-year lease for grazing rights on all but the twenty acres surrounding the house. But Big Joe, sensing your father's vulnerable condition, began an intensified campaign to coerce Bill into selling out. Your dad still refused to sell the ranch, even after the loss of his family. Then Big Joe claimed to be your biological father. Shortly afterward, Bill moved to Portland. I don't know whether or not he believed the part about not being your father, or if it was only the realization he'd been so drunk, he wasn't there for Kathryn that night. Whatever demons played with his mind, they kept him from reaching out to you, and your loss from his life tormented him."

"Did my father tell you that he believed what happened was consensual?"

"He didn't, but then the scenario explained the strange distance between him and your mother following that night. I was contacted by Big Joe's attorney a few weeks after the reading of your father's will. The paperwork claiming paternity included a DNA lab report."

"Why would you believe a DNA report that he could easily have falsified, the way he did in JD's case?"

"I don't believe him, but JD had indisputable proof to counter his claim. Still, I'm surprised he would claim to have had a relationship with your mother."

"What about JD, Bob? Have you heard anything from him since the revelations back in August from Hiram Stokes?"

"Communications on that front have been strangely quiet for the last four months."

"Do me a couple of favors: see what you can find out about JD and call Susan Hoffman to ask if she'll see me. Check on the whereabouts of Big Joe, and then give me a call on my cell."

"What are you up to, Casey?"

"You don't want to know. Let's just say that I'm getting all my ducks in a row, and Big Mouth Joe Gannon will rue the day he tangled with me."

******

Portland was warmer than Casey had expected, but it was raining cats and dogs when she exited the terminal. George nearly squeezed the life out of her with his exuberant hug. "Howdy, Sis! About time you came for a visit."

Casey protested George taking her two bags and Susan latching onto her carry-on, but gave up when Susan kissed her on the cheek. "Welcome to Portland, Casey. We were so sorry to hear of your grandmother's passing."

Casey couldn't do more than acknowledge the condolences with a nod. Gram's loss was too fresh, and the wounds far from healed.

She caved when Susan and George each had a litter of kittens because she was intending to set up in a nearby motel. Casey spent the next three weeks getting her first glimpse of the Pacific Ocean and the Cascade Mountains while they waited for the lab to come back with the DNA comparison of George and herself.

Susan agreed it was the best way to thwart Big Joe. "No wonder Bill was so tormented. He never really got over the nightmares and flashbacks, but throughout all the years of therapy, he never mentioned anything regarding your being anything but his daughter."

"I sure hope this test proves George and I are related."

"What are you going to do if the test upholds his claim?"

"It won't make much difference. I'm going after that creep."

Casey could tell by Susan's expression that she was reading between the lines and was grateful that her stepmother didn't ask any more questions. If—more likely when—law enforcement got around to questioning Susan, she wouldn't have to lie.

The long-awaited results sent Casey back to Colorado to confer with Bob Jackson, who had interrupted their family get-together.

Susan gave it her best shot to delay Casey's departure. "Stay a few days longer, so we can discuss a plan of action."

"There is little that can be accomplished here, but I promise to keep you informed. I have several ad campaigns and websites near completion. I need to consult with those clients. It's time for me to go home."

George set the larger pieces of Casey's luggage near the check-in scale, and turned to her. "Is Colorado home now?"

"No. I'm not sure it ever will be, but I need to run this lab report by Bob Jackson." She gave her half-brother a peck on the cheek and was enveloped in another bear hug.

Susan's hug was every bit as warm, but a heck of a lot easier on her ribs.

******

Casey couldn't unwind or relax during the flight or on the limo ride to Bob's office. Ken was her driver, which brought back memories of her first trip here and the first time in her memory that she'd met Captain JD Gannon or, as her grandmother had called him, Jimmy. JD was the subject of the call she'd received from Bob, but he didn't want to discuss what he'd found out over the phone. So here she was, stuck once more in rush hour traffic moving at a snail's pace through Denver. Somehow the whole feel of the evening rush seemed different, and like the impending winter darkness, she shuddered as she felt a dark, malevolent shadow block the sun from her life.

It was the same kind of terror that haunted her recurring nightmare. Susan had heard her in the throes of the dream and noticed the light shining beneath the guestroom door. Casey was frantically sketching and hadn't heard the faint knock or noticed Susan enter the room. Casey wondered, as Ken pulled up in front of the building that housed the law office, if Susan was correct and the sketches of her shadow man were really of her father.

She entered to find Bob waiting to escort her to his office. Ken must have called up when he'd gone to park. He'd assured her it was best to leave her luggage in the limo. Once seated in Bob's office, he began with the results of her trip to see Susan.

"How was your stay in Portland?"

"I guess you'd say productive." She tossed the lab report onto the table.

Bob scanned it carefully. "You must be relieved to know that Bill was indeed your father."

Casey didn't want to admit that she ever doubted the results. "I won't be relieved until Big Joe is in jail or six feet under."

"As your attorney, Casey, I have to caution you not to tell others that you are planning on taking revenge on Big Joe."

"Well, as my attorney, find out what I can do to file fraud charges or something, for his manipulating official lab reports."

"I'm not sure we can do much to prove intentional manipulation."

"Try. We have documentation of the attack on my person and on the false paternity claim. Not to mention the falsified DNA reports on JD and me. I also want the remainder of the lease on my father's ranch revoked."

"This could get pricey. Big Joe isn't going to give up without a fight."

"You keep telling me I am a wealthy woman. So, go earn some of it. I'll sign a warrant or whatever to bring that creep to justice. Now, tell me what you found out about JD."

Bob gave her a wait-one-moment gesture and pressed the intercom on his desk. "Mary, has O'Bannon arrived?" Mary answered in the affirmative and admitted a man with the build of an NFL linebacker. Introductions were made.

"Casey, this is Sergeant Rick O'Bannon."

She stood to get a better perspective as he approached. His hand was warm as he grasped hers, but made her appendage appear that of a small child in contrast. He was nearly as tall as JD, but at that point the physical comparison differed. His hazel eyes twinkled at her blatant assessment. The man looked like the blond actor who played Hercules on the old TV series, but with a short military buzz cut. She extricated her hand from his grip, nodded, and simply replied, "Sergeant." She gave Bob a questioning look as she reoccupied her seat, and the sergeant squeezed into the beige leather armchair next to hers.

Bob began to fill her in. "At your request, I began looking into the strange silence regarding both of our attempts to contact JD. I was unable to communicate with him, but Sergeant O'Bannon contacted me while you were in Portland. I will let him tell you the rest of the news."

"Oh, God! Has JD been killed?"

"No. The Captain is still among the living, but he was severely wounded and has been unconscious from the time he was transported from rubble of the battlefield in Iraq until five days before Christmas."

"Why didn't he let me know where he was?"

"The Captain has been in and out of surgery several times since then. Once he was off life support and the feeding tube was removed, they began to work on rebuilding his shattered hip. He was heavily medicated when I last saw him. However, he was coherent enough to order me to check on your welfare and whereabouts. A friend of yours, Bonnie, said you'd flown to Denver on a personal matter. The Captain ordered me to contact this office and to speak only with Bob Jackson."

Casey processed what she'd just heard and wondered if Big Joe had anything to do with what happened to JD. "Did you report back to him on your findings?"

"I did, and he booked a flight for me to come here. My orders are to return with you in tow."

"Has anyone other than you been to see him?"

"I was told by one of the day nurses that when he was first in ICU and still unconscious, he was visited by his father"

"His father passed away." Casey made the mental leap; it had to have been Big Joe. That would account for his mysterious absence when she was here before her trip to Portland.

"Fortunately, JD's records showed his father was deceased, and the imposter wasn't admitted. I assume it was Big Joe; at that point, all he had to do was pull the plug." Rick noted the emotions that crossed her face.

Casey's penetrating green eyes pinned Bob to his chair. "Find a way to get Big Joe within the law, or you'll be defending me. He is going down, even if I have to end him on my own." She turned to JD's fellow marine. "What time is our flight?"

"I have to book return tickets. We weren't sure how soon you would return from Portland, or what your response would be. Both Bob and JD warned me you could be unpredictable."

She filed his comment away. Maybe JD didn't know her as well as he'd made her think. Gram could have told them her reaction to the unfolding events was completely consistent with her sense of justice and willingness to fight for it.

Rick O'Bannon was a wealth of information and filled in the blanks for her since she'd last seen JD.

******

Casey thought she was prepared to visit JD, but the sight of him flat on his back, pale, thin, wrapped in bandages, hooked up to monitors and IVs rattled her. She squelched the urge to cry when she walked into the room with Rick O'Bannon. One look at the curvy blonde nurse with the soft blue eyes decided her approach. "Well, Jimmy boy, it's easy to see why you would forget to let me know that you were home, alive, and relatively in one piece. Been too busy checking out all the sympathetic nurses?"

Rick snorted, trying without success to subdue the urge to laugh. He followed the affronted nurse out of the ICU.

She sat in the large green vinyl-clad armchair near his bed. Scooting it closer, she assessed him. "You look pretty spaced out, JD. Do you even know who I am?"

He looked her up and down, lingering overly long on her chest area. "Umm, Sandy? No. Laura, right?" he replied in a hoarse whisper that appeared deadly serious.

At that response, she silently berated herself, what the hell, am I doing here? Aggravated with herself Casey gave him a piece of her mind. "I thought that you ordered your marine buddy to bring me here? Now, you don't even know who the hell I am." She rose from her chair. "See yah around, JD. I hope you get out of here soon."

"Don't go, Cassie!"

His voice halted her in her tracks; it was scratchy and sounded painful. She walked back and looked down at him, reaching for a tissue on the bedside table. No one in her memory other than JD called her Cassie. She leaned over to soak up the tears leaking down toward each temple and his mummy-like bandages.

"I didn't forget you, Cassie. I was only retaliating for the sympathetic nurse crack." His voice was failing him, and he wasn't sure he'd got all of the words out clearly until she responded.

"Yeah? Well, maybe if you'd kept in touch I could see the humor in your wisecrack, but you didn't. You turned your back on me exactly like my father did, and it hurt."

He tried to mouth a response, but his vocal cords would no longer respond. The machines monitoring every change in his condition began to beep and buzz. They registered even more agitation when the on duty nurse barreled through the door to check on him and chased Cassie out of the while she sedated him. *Please, Cassie, come back!* His mind called out right before the sedative sent him back into darkness.

******

Casey's dreams took on a new urgency, as did her sketched documentations of the nightshades that remained elusive. Susan swore that the shadow man in the sketches looked like Casey's father. She made the trip to the Virginia VA Hospital once a week, for eight months, occasionally staying over an extra day and working on designs for clients from a nearby hotel room.

Once JD's bandages were removed and he began therapy to regain his strength, she looked again at the sketches of the shadow man from her dreams. The man she was so desperate to reach looked more like the post-Iraq JD who was struggling to acclimate himself to a reconstructed right hip. She wondered if her shadow man was a composite of both her father and JD. Casey consciously made an effort to concentrate on the bear-like silhouette, which obstructed a clear image of the man in her dreams.

For eight months, she visited him, and he always asked if she would return the following week. Instead of their relationship improving, however, as he got stronger, it deteriorated. He was uncommunicative, edgy, and jumped all over her case when he found out she had pressed charges against Big Joe for fraud and extortion. She assumed Rick O'Bannon was the big mouth who'd filled him in on that little tidbit. She'd made it clear to Bob Jackson that JD was not to be informed of her efforts to attack Big Joe legally. Casey decided that given his state of agitation, she would keep her mission to revoke the lease on her parents' ranch behind closed lips.

His doctors and psychologists attributed his behavior to PTSD. They also made a point of how relieved they were with the results of his brain scans, and there didn't appear to be detectable damage. The doctors were reluctant to give her much detail since she was not a member of his immediate family.

She was devastated when she went to see him the second week of September and found him gone. He'd been released and had gone home to Colorado, and he'd never even called her!

Chapter 10 (Part Two) May 31, 2009

Casey took one final tour of the small house that had been home for most of her life. She waited until the moving van pulled away before locking the door for the last time. The new owners would be taking possession on June first. The keys and garage opener that she dropped off with the real estate agent had all the trauma of severing the lifeline of a newborn. Solace awaited her in the form of her equine pals. Casey dug down deep into her drying-up well of inner strength to pull herself back together as she fueled up the dependable Yukon. Then she headed to Bonnie's farm to hook up her newly acquired horse trailer.

Andi was pacing the pavement near the line of parked trailers when Casey pulled in the drive at the boarding stable. The hyper brunette quickly added her traveling cases to Casey's, which were already stashed in the cargo area. Her friend settled down once the trailer was hooked and the light checks completed. Bucky and his new buddy Chief were loaded. Casey had rescued Chief from a trip to the renders to be a companion for Bucky when she'd decided to sell the house and relocate.

Both women were dressed in boot-cut denims, scruffy well-worn western boots, and heavyweight gray hoodies that covered similar red T-shirts. However, that was where the similarities ended.

Friends since high school, the girls had always presented an interesting contrast. Black natural curls, dark brown eyes, and hourglass figure aside, Andi, was warm, outgoing, and a hugger. She smiled perpetually, and flirting came as natural as breathing.

Casey worried about her friend plopping back onto the drive as she hung out the passenger side window waving to Bonnie and the boarders assembled to document their departure. "Bye! Take care of Sissy for me."

"Let us know when you get there." Bonnie yelled. "In fact, let us know when you stop for the night!"

"Lord almighty, it is going to take us hours to make all the requested calls," Casey complained as she steered the rig down the winding drive toward the state route.

Andi giggled. "Well, at least you know you have people who care about you. I'll call my mom, and we can post on my Facebook page. That'll cover most of our friends, my brother, and Bonnie too. You know she'll clue in her cousin Chuck."

A short mile and a quarter down the road, she aimed her version of an ark in the direction of the Interstate. "I guess that will help some. I still have to let Millie know where we are and check in with Bob Jackson. Then there's my buttinsky stepmother; none of those folks are into social media."

"You only have yourself to blame for that. You invited Susan into your life by spilling the beans about your feud with Big Joe."

That was one thing Casey didn't want to think about while playing dodgem down the Interstate with Andi, Bucky, and Chief all counting on her to chauffeur them safely to Eastern Colorado. She changed the subject. "Are you okay with leaving Sissy in someone else's care for a couple of weeks?"

"She isn't in just anyone's care! Bonnie is looking after her."

"What did the vet say about her tendon?"

"Sissy is finished as a riding horse. Her reoccurring problems from the injuries as a result of her years as a racehorse have taken their toll. Doc Steadman thinks she'll be able support a foal okay, though. Bonnie and I have purchased a stallion's services, and Doc is doing the artificial insemination. Sissy can remain at home while trying to become a mommy."

"It's lucky thing you have that option; a gelding would be done for." She thought about the two horses following them down the highway and turned her attention fully to the task at hand.

Andi dropped the chitchat, started some tunes, and began texting the friends they'd just left behind. Casey had blocked her out, and Andi knew from a long past history when that happened, there was as much chance of getting conversation out of a stone.

"We're about midway through Indiana, Andi. See if you can locate a truck stop."

"There's one two exits up," she said.

Casey pulled the trailer to the far end of the truck parking area after filling up the tank.

"I'm so weak from hunger that it was a struggle lifting the water bucket to give Chief a drink," Andi grumbled as she slid into the first empty booth and snatched up one of the menus stashed behind the napkin holder on the faux walnut table before Casey even sat down.

"You must have a tapeworm. We stopped twice for pit stops. You bought snacks and drinks at each place! You ought to have that checked out."

"How much further to our overnight stop?"

"We should be able to make our horse motel reservations in another four or five hours. So stock up on your travel snacks. No more meals until we check in, and the horses are settled for the night" Casey laughed at her friend's loud exaggerated groan and went to work on a cup of great-smelling vegetable soup and a turkey club sandwich.

Horses safely settled for the night, both girls hit their e-mail and made the obligatory phone calls. Casey contacted Bob Jackson to inform him of their location and estimated time of arrival at the ranch.

"I will notify Ben Rodriguez. He'll have the stalls ready for the horses and some groceries in for you."

"Thanks Bob."

"Do you want me to notify JD also?"

"I don't think that's a good idea. I don't want to see him any more than he wants to see me. My intention is to sell the place once I get rid of the Big Joe threat. If JD wants to buy me out, that's fine by me."

"Where will you go, Casey?"

"Probably back to Ohio." She terminated the call, and then turned to her friend. "Andi, let's find some dinner."

They ended up at a pancake house an exit down the interstate. Andi's curiosity got the better of her. "Casey, what happened between you and JD? I thought the two of you had a thing going."

"What would make you think that?"

"Well…for starters, there was the third degree he gave all of us when we went to the sale where you bought Bucky. And there were the hot looks he kept giving you."

"That was three years ago, and you tend to let your imagination get the better of you."

"Don't give me that, Casey, I saw the rain video on the Internet."

Casey was sure the clip had circulated compliments of Big Joe Gannon. "JD changed a lot after he came home from Iraq. In

September of 07, I arrived at the VA in Virginia to find he'd been released. He had gone home to Colorado without so much as a goodbye, drop dead, or go to hell. I haven't heard from him in well over a year.

"Did you try to call him?"

"No. He knew how to reach me if he wanted to."

Casey was grateful when Andi dropped the subject of JD. His about-face had been strange, and she was tired of trying to figure it out. She needed rest for the long haul yet to come, and prayed she had a dreamless night for a change.

Chapter 11

JD had waited and prayed for Cassie to come home since he was in his young teens, and now that she was on her way, he was dreading the thought. He wiped the sweat from his eyes, tied the blue bandana around his head, and finished pitching the hay from a flatbed down to Ben and Rick, who were stacking it inside the pole barn that once more had stalls to house horses.

"I don't know about you guys, but this Chicago boy needs a break and a cold one."

JD figured Rick was calling a break more for his former captain's benefit than for himself. "Twenty minutes," JD reluctantly agreed. "We need to finish before it really gets hot."

Ben grabbed a bottle of water from the cooler on the back porch, tossed one to JD, and handed a can of Coors to Rick. He shook his head at the other man's choice of hydration "You know that stuff is only going to make you sweat more."

"You're talking to a guy that spent three tours in the desert of Iraq. This is cool by comparison."

JD knew Rick had it right The welcome break was an indication of how much further he had to go before he was in shape again. He tossed the empty plastic bottle in the trash barrel that was set up between the new manufactured home being erected and the back of the ranch house. Today was day three that the crew had been there erecting the new structure.

Rick shook his head as they walked back toward the barn, pulling on their work gloves. "Do you suppose your little green-eyed spitfire is going to throw us out of the house and make us live in that?"

"I doubt it. She's probably intends to occupy it herself."

"Why in the hell would she do that, JD?"

He merely shrugged, climbed up onto the truck to begin pitching hay, and thought about his last discussion with Bob Jackson. "She isn't planning to stay on the ranch, JD. Casey told me she wants to sell the place when she gets rid of the threat of Big Joe." That intent worried JD, it was his incentive to stay put where he was.

JD showered and then assessed his bearded reflection in the steamy mirror over the double sink in the now completed master bathroom. The burn scars on the right side of his jaw weren't as visible with addition of a beard, and it was easier to trim the facial hair than to shave over the scarred tissue. Skin grafts had helped smooth the worst burns on his face and neck. There wasn't much he could do about damage to his right shoulder and upper arm. His clothing covered most of the healed wounds, but the real damage couldn't be camouflaged. He woke with cold sweats, disorientated and not sure where he was. He looked for insurgents lurking behind every outcropping or building, and every piece of road litter became a roadside bomb. Rick was the only one who could reach him or handle him when he went around the bend. His old sergeant had taken him more than once to the VA clinic for his periodic evaluation.

He'd broken ties with Cassie when the extent of his mental issues became apparent. It was his worst fear that he might put her in danger should he become violent. He knew she didn't want any part of the ranch, but now her need for revenge brought her back to confront Big Joe.

The sound of another truck approaching sidetracked his speculation of how Cassie would react to his altered physical appearance and his lack of mental stability. He was relieved to find it wasn't another hay delivery, but a moving van that postponed his much-needed afternoon nap.

One of the movers approached JD as he stepped onto the back porch. "You Ben Rodriguez?"

"No, I'm JD Gannon. Ben takes care of the ranch when I'm away."

"We've a houseful of furniture to deliver for a…" He consulted his iPad. "Cassandra Hoffman. Where do you want us to put it?" The mover cast an inquisitive eye at the nearly completed structure sixty feet off the main house.

JD didn't have a clue what she wanted done with her belongings, and if Ben did, he'd not shared the information. Rick and Ben had gone to town for provisions that were bound to include more beer. "Just unload it into the large room to the right as you enter." He waved, indicating the door behind him. JD unhooked the restraints on the screen door that kept it from swinging too far open if the wind caught it. He used the iron boot scraper to prop the door flush to the back of the house near the small kitchen window, allowing full use of the entry for the movers. "Miss Hoffman can decide where she wants things when she arrives."

He signed for the delivery after a cursory inspection of the packed boxes and furniture on the inventory list dated June third. Once the moving van left, JD limped toward the bedroom and sprawled across the bed. His new artificial hip was giving him fits, but he counted himself lucky. He still had his leg, unlike many others who'd been in the VA hospital or attended the outpatient clinic. He closed his eyes and pictured Cassie the last time he'd seen her.

He'd been puffing like an old fashion steam engine and soaked in his own sweat when she'd strolled into the therapy room with Rick. His bandages, much lighter at that point, still covered his face and neck, but his hair was growing and covering up the scar from the procedure to relieve the pressure on his brain. Her green eyes roved over his disheveled self, and she smiled as if he had just run a marathon. It hurt his pride that she saw him in such a state, but at the same time he wanted to wrap her in his arms. He'd growled at her about arriving unannounced and disrupting his routine. Her green eyes flashed anger and hurt as she whipped around and exited the room. That was the last time he'd seen her. He'd turned tail and run home before her next visit. In a few days, he was going to have to face her or leave her on her own to take on their mutual nemesis alone.

JD drifted off to sleep weighing his chances of protecting her from Big Joe.

******

JD, Rick, and Ben were relaxing on the back porch and taking in the sunset following a carryout rib, fries, and slaw dinner. JD worked on another cup of coffee while his companions downed their second can of beer. Never a beer drinker, his friend's choice of brew didn't tempt him, but there were times that a bracing scotch would sure hit the spot. It sure wasn't an option while taking Vicodin and other meds that were required to manage the pain of his wounded body and mind, unless he wanted to end it all.

The trio looked toward the access road as a trail of dust worked its way closer the ranch. The two vehicles emerging from the thick, billowing tan cloud appeared to be a couple of sheriff's transports.

Ben didn't like the looks of it. "What the hell do you think they want?"

JD was wondering the same thing: it was unusual to get a call from the law out here, and seldom did it require more than one deputy. "I don't know, but it looks like they sure have a burr under their saddle blanket!"

The three occupants appeared to be kicking back on the rear porch of the faded frame ranch, watching the sunset and working on a couple of long necks. Nothing could be farther from the truth; they monitored the approach of the sheriff and two deputies and were ready to spring into action at the slightest provocation. The two deputies were unfamiliar to them, but each was familiar with Sheriff William Tucker. Tucker's paunch hung over his belt and jiggled as he swaggered toward them from the marked Cherokee. He was flanked by the two younger deputies who'd parked an older version of the Jeep model directly behind the leader of the small invasion force.

J.D. knew Tucker from their high school days, and he appeared to have found his calling. He hadn't liked the class bully then, and he didn't like the man that Big Joe had singlehandedly financed and installed as sheriff in the last bogus election. Rick rose from his seat and moved to open the screen door. JD didn't move from his seat. "To what do we owe this visit, Billy? I'm sure it isn't a social call, since you brought backup."

Tucker didn't like being called Billy in such a sarcastic tone. He decided to exert some authority. He was almost as tall as JD and had at least a hundred pounds on him these days, but he was still intimidated by the cold blue eyes that pierced the aviator sunglasses that hid his own mud-brown orbs. Mirrored glasses tended to intimidate a lot of folks, but not this bunch. He glanced over at the opened door. "Where the hell do you think you're going? This is an official call, and I have some questions for all of you."

Rick gave him a look that left little doubt the sheriff was an insignificant disruption in his day. "I have to take a piss, and I don't need anyone's permission to do it."

The big blond hulk had an attitude that dared the lawman to make an issue of his entering the house. "Hurry it up. I don't have all night." Then Sheriff Tucker removed his sunglasses as he leaned against the post at the porch entry near where JD was still seated. Ben had removed his boots from the rail where he'd been teetering on the back legs of his white plastic chair. Tucker stuffed his glasses in his front shirt pocket, and then discreetly—he thought—he nodded his head. The two deputies moved to either side of the porch, effectively flanking the remaining occupants of the porch. A lot braver now, he brought up the reason for the call.

"Where were you this afternoon, around three, JD?"

"I've been here all day."

"Can you prove it?"

"If I have to. Why don't you quit beating around the bush, and just spit it out?"

"Someone took a shot at Big Joe. He was on his way back home from the capitol when a shot took out two tires on his limo, and another went through the rear side door."

JD knew what Billy was thinking. He'd been so close so Big Joe the last couple of years that his nose had a decidedly brown tinge. "Is he dead?"

"No, but he's hospitalized with serious injuries."

"So…what does that have to do with me?"

"Big Joe named you as a prime suspect in his assassination attempt, followed by someone named Cassandra Hoffman."

JD's hip shot a pain through his entire body as his chair went flying behind him and he grabbed Billy Tucker by the front of his uniform, effectively crushing his aviators. His cat-like move caught the Sheriff off guard, and he never had time to reach for his handgun. It was a good thing the Sheriff didn't make the mistake of reaching for it. JD was fighting the urge to end him.

"JD, turn him loose," Rick said, as he stepped up behind the deputy who'd taken up a position on the eastern side of the porch. JD's friend and former sergeant had worked his way around from the front of the house to disarm the unsuspecting deputy in the quickly fading dusk.

Ben quietly held out his hand to collect the firearm from the deputy at the other end of the porch while JD was disarming Billy. Once the sheriff found his voice again, he served JD with a search warrant. Rick stepped in to accompany the sheriff and his deputies around the house, the barn, and the new home that was almost completed.

Sheriff Tucker appeared disappointed he hadn't found any incriminating evidence, and that every one of them could account for their whereabouts that afternoon. Casey wasn't even in Colorado yet. That pretty much eliminated her.

"Face it, Sheriff." JD told him, "If one of us took a shot at Big Joe, he'd be dead. I'm sure he has a long list of people who would be willing to put an end to him."

"I'll be checking up on your alibis, and if they can't be verified, I'll also have an arrest warrant to serve."

JD squared off again eye-to-eye with the sheriff, who was covered with sweat like it was mid-afternoon instead of a cool star filled night. "If you come back here, Billy, a word of advice: bring more reinforcements."

Rick pulled a Glock from the waistband at the small of his back. He kept it trained on the retreating vehicles until they began to fade into the dark landscape. "You think he'll be dense enough to come back, JD?"

JD retrieved his upturned coffee mug and the newly detached handle before entering the house. "I don't think Billy will be back, but when he reports to Big Joe, expect some sort of reprisal. Stay alert and armed. If Big Joe thinks one of us tried to take him out, Tucker's visit tonight won't be the end of it." He cast a questioning look at his friend and former sergeant.

Rick shrugged his broad shoulders in reply to the unasked question; Ben's dark eyes were just as enigmatic.

Sleep was a long time coming to JD. He struggled with sorting out daily life from the reruns of war, and the sheriff's visit didn't help in quelling the persistent flashbacks.

Chapter 12

Casey and Andi discussed the news relayed to them earlier that Thursday afternoon by Bob Jackson while waiting for their dinner orders.

"Who do you think made a move to take out Big Joe?" Andi was giving her taciturn traveling companion the third degree. She knew Casey had already spent a large portion of her inheritance on lawyers and private investigators. Could her friend have also hired an assassin to speed up the slow process of pursuing legal avenues to address her grievances? "You think that JD or one of his friends took matters into their own hands yesterday?"

"I doubt that, Andi; you haven't met Rick O'Bannon. If he or JD went after Big Joe, the slimeball would be history. Big Joe's wealth and power wouldn't deter either of them, and he would already be polluting the groundwater."

"Aha…Casey…you wouldn't have anything to do with the attack on him, would you?"

Casey tightened her jaw and bided her time until the waitress departed. She contemplated Andi's question while absently drawing random patterns with a French fry in the blob of catsup she'd just squirted onto her plate. "If I did have a hand at trying to end him, I sure wouldn't admit to it."

"Why? Do you think I would blab it around?"

Casey rolled her eyes and decided to let the obvious answer to that question go unanswered. No point in insulting her best friend. "There are probably legions of suspects in addition to me that would interest investigators." Andi appeared to be placated, and the remainder of the meal was spent plotting the course from the Lincoln area to their destination. Both women were as road-weary as Bucky and Chief. A day driving through rain with occasional thunderstorms had severely shortened tempers.

Casey's morning wasn't progressing any better than her interminable sleepless night. The same old troublesome dreams assaulted her whenever she dozed off. It seemed the closer she got to Eastern Colorado, the more frequent and intense the nightmares became.

Arms braced on the front of the shower stall, her head bent forward, Casey began to relax as the warm water pelted her back, and the tears that mingled with the overhead spray subsided. She sighed, wrapped a towel around her, and finished preparing for the new day. Casey tried to control the deep, penetrating sense of loss and loneliness that invaded her shivering body. Thanks to the strong coffee and aspirin that Andi managed to scrounge up, along with a couple of great tasting apricot Danishes, her throbbing head began to subside. Andi noticed her friend's swollen and bloodshot eyes as the two packed up in preparation to check out of the motel. "Are you okay, Casey?"

"Oh…yeah. Just feeling sorry for myself. I haven't felt this awful emptiness since I was a little kid and lost my family. I really will be alone once you return home. Let's feed the horses. We can get breakfast and fuel up the Yukon for the rest of the trip while they're chowing down."

Things went downhill following the topping off of the tank. The front right tire on the trailer was flat as the pancakes that they had eaten an hour or so earlier. Three hours later, the repaired tire securely in place and the trailer hooked up, it was time to load their equine charges. Bucky staged a revolt. Legs braced, he refused to budge. Even after Chief was loaded, it took another thirty minutes to convince him to join his traveling companion.

Casey leaned against the trailer door after securing it. "I knew I should've crawled back between the sheets and merely forgotten about today."

Andi shook her head and climbed into the passenger seat. Her mom always said that things like this came in threes, but she didn't think Casey would appreciate hearing that saying repeated at the moment. So she stretched her willpower, buttoned her lip, and kept quiet.

Only an hour out from the ranch, they were pulled over by the local sheriff. He demanded her license, registration, health certificates for the horses, and then his stupid questions started.

Number three! Andi thought and bit her lip to keep from verbalizing it. She would swear to people for years that she could see the steam radiating from her friend as Casey tried to control her temper and irritation with the obnoxious law official. "How long have you been in Colorado, Miss Hoffman?"

Casey didn't like this portly lawman who hid behind mirrored sunglasses. "This time, only a couple of hours."

"Big Joe Gannon named you as a primary suspect in the attempt on his life."

"Are you arresting me, sheriff?"

"No, not at this time. I'm checking all strangers and suspicious characters."

"How commendable." Bucky punctuated her sarcastic remark with a loud snort and a thump on the trailer. "Well, if you're not cuffing me or hauling me off to the clink, and I don't need to call my attorney, I suggest you let us proceed. Unless you want a couple very tired, irritated horses trashing the trailer and staging an escape."

He handed back her license and other paperwork. Then a parting threat: "I'll be keeping an eye on you, along with the rest of the inhabitants on your place."

Casey smiled her sweetest. "How reassuring."

It was early evening by the time she parked the rig near the barn. Not a soul showed up to greet them or help with the unloading of the horses.

"It's spooky how quiet it is around here." Andi's take on the deserted feel to the ranch didn't escape Casey either. She escorted Bucky to the round pen that she'd ordered, and Ben had erected. She continued to scan their surroundings, but didn't comment until the horses were safely turned out.

"I expected Ben to be here. Even with the delays we suffered, he knew we were due today." She tried Ben's phone. "That's strange." After leaving a message that they had arrived on his voicemail, the pair watered the horses and threw them some hay.

"I'm starving!"

"Well, let's unpack the essentials and the groceries we picked up in the last town. I can't have you passing out from hunger, Andi. You're going to need your strength to help me move in the contents of the moving van that brought the furniture and household items."

Casey parked the Yukon in front of the new structure and unloaded the bare minimum of their luggage, much as they had for the overnight stays in motels on the trip from Ohio. It felt like they weren't the first to set foot in the modest manufactured home. She wondered if the obnoxious sheriff had been in her new home. The groceries were placed onto the kitchen counter next to the fridge.

A tour of their new digs was in order before unpacking and storing the contents. They backtracked toward the small foyer where they'd entered.

"I chose this model because of the huge great room at the front." Casey opened the door to the left of the large entry. "It wasn't difficult to split the room to accommodate space for my studio and still have a decent size living room."

The studio, like the living room and the center hall, had laminated oak flooring. The entryway, the utility room to the right across from the studio, the kitchen at the back of the house, and both baths were ceramic tiled in an off-white and pale green. The bedrooms were the only rooms with low pile, darker green carpeting.

Andi scrunched up her nose. "You develop a thing for greens when I wasn't looking?"

"This is probably the only green we're likely to see around this place."

The microwave, range, and fridge were all functional. They shared their first meal seated on the kitchen floor with their legs crossed and backs propped against the cabinets while balancing plates on their laps. "I think we'll have to unpack the sleeping bags for tonight," Casey sighed. She was too exhausted to think about searching out the contents of the moving van to set up the beds.

"That's fine with me, as long as we sleep on the softer carpeted floor."

"Deal. Let's go find a stall for the horses, bed them down, and feed them. Then we can call it a night."

******

The sun was at its peak, and the two women were sweltering as they worked at ferrying Casey's belongings from the ranch house to her newly constructed home.

"It's strange no one is around." Andi thought it was eerie that not a soul had shown up at the ranch since their arrival the evening before, and Casey still could not reach Ben on his phone.

"How about some lunch? I could use a break and a tall glass of tea." Casey hoped that the ice-maker on the fridge had been busy producing cubes while they were straining every muscle in their bodies and soaking their T-shirts and cut-offs with sweat.

Lunch out of the way, they decided to put the horses back into their stalls during the heat of the day. On the way back toward the house, a silver pickup came roaring up the drive, spewing dust into the clear blue, nearly obscuring the rays of the sun. Casey recognized Rick as the driver, and he really looked pissed.

The three-quarter-ton Ram shuddered and swayed on its wheels from the impact as the driver side door slammed against its rugged body. Ben exited the passenger side with considerably more respect for the vehicle. His demeanor was somber, but he appeared to be in a better frame of mind than his companion.

Casey walked up and shook his hand. "Ben, this is my friend Andi. We've been worried about you. I haven't been able to reach you, and we were thinking all sorts awful things."

He accompanied the women back toward the house where Rick had recently disappeared behind the screen door that surprisingly was still on its hinges. "I'm sorry about that, Casey, but the sheriff confiscated our phones when he locked us up yesterday morning."

"Why did he arrest you?"

"We had a run-in with him and a couple of deputies a few days ago. Rick and JD got a little testy with the lawmen."

"I know about that run-in and the reason for the sheriff's visit. Bob Jackson gave me a heads-up. Did the sheriff think the two of you tried to off Big Joe?"

"He might think it, but there isn't any proof. We were arrested on our way out of the VA hospital, after checking on JD. We were charged with assaulting officers of the law."

Casey wondered why JD was back in a VA facility, but she wasn't going to ask. "How did you get sprung?"

"Rick used his one call to inform Bob Jackson of the situation, and he posted bail. He vouched for us, and JD, but we're still facing charges in court."

"Well…I came real close to joining you. I don't think that I've ever run into a more sinister individual."

"When did you meet him?"

"He stopped us about fifty miles out from here yesterday."

"Don't say anything to Rick or JD about that encounter. It was his threat toward you that set JD off and started the whole confrontation."

Casey didn't say anything more after agreeing not to mention the incident upon their arrival the previous day. She had a gut feeling that Bob had glossed over the confrontation at the ranch when he sketched out the incident, or he didn't know the extent of what happened either.

With the help of the two men, the furniture was moved from the main house and put in place in no time. Casey offered to buy dinner for her moving crew. "Give us a chance to clean up, and you guys can decide where to eat. We also need to stock up on some groceries, so you can show us where we can accomplish that little chore."

There was a bit of an altercation about who would drive, but Casey relented when Rick told her that she didn't know where she was going. She won out on taking the Yukon for transporting the grocery purchases to prevent having the eggs scrambled from bouncing around in the bed of the pickup.

The steak house was on the order of a typical western motif associated with that type of restaurant, but the food was excellent. The conversation, however, didn't help Casey's digestion. She ended up in a heated discussion due to her refusal to accompany Rick on his trip to the VA Hospital the next day. "I'm way behind on my work and have several commissions that are due within the next 10 days. Also, I have a friend visiting."

"Damn it, Casey, you know she could come with us. We could do some sightseeing, and hit some tourist spots afterward."

Andi was hoping to smooth things over. "That sounds like fun, and I would like to see JD again. Please, Casey, can't we go?"

"You can go, if you want, but I have a lot to do."

"Come on, Casey, don't you want to mend fences with JD?"

"No. He made his choice, and I'm fine with it. You'll enjoy the tour, and most of the time Rick is excellent company."

Chapter 13

JD was chilling in the obligatory wheelchair in the solarium when Rick arrived. One quick glance at him, and Rick knew his former captain was ready to rip into him. Thank you, Casey, he thought. JD settled down as soon as he saw Casey's friend in his company. "JD, you know Andi?"

"Sure. It's been a few years, but you're still a real knockout."

She went over to kiss him on the cheek. "JD you're such a charmer. I really don't know how Casey can resist you!"

"She knows me better than you do."

Rick could hear the pain and longing in JD's voice, and it hadn't escaped his notice that he'd immediately looked past them when they entered. The first few moments, he scanned the doorway in search of one more visitor. His disappointment was palpable. Rick could tell that JD really wanted to ask about Casey, but he directed his inquiries to their recent trek. "Did you encounter any difficulties on the highway?"

Andi had been warned not to tell JD or Rick about the run-in with the local sheriff. She spun an entertaining account of their travels. "And other than bouts with the weather, we had a flat on the trailer early morning of the day we arrived, and then Bucky refused to load. As a result, we pulled in later than expected, and there wasn't a soul around."

Rick and JD knew she was hiding something. Silent communication that had been honed between them over the years assigned the gathering of intelligence to Rick.

******

Some enemy was clawing around in JD's skull, and creepy crawlies were swarming around inside his body, attempting to chew their way out through his skin. The meds were wearing off. The medication had been given to combat the flashbacks and hallucinations that were part of his PTSD, but they brought their own kind of torture.

He'd been confined for ten days thanks to Rick carting his ass to the VA after he tried to choke Billy Tucker. He counted himself lucky that his hip didn't need replaced and that he hadn't end up in lockup with the others. His thought was interrupted by Rick's entrance.

His friend was here to drive him home, but Rick was far too perceptive. "Christ, JD, you look like shit warmed over! Have you taken your meds today?"

The only way JD could get the SOB to drive him home was to take the meds that he hated. They dulled his mind and, from his perspective, put him at a disadvantage. He couldn't shake the feeling they were all in the crosshairs.

"Look, JD, I don't think it's a good idea for you to go back to your place alone. I could move my stuff over there."

"No. You need to stay at the ranch to keep an eye on the place and the two women."

"Do you think the sheriff or one of Big Joe's other minions will try something before our court date?"

"I wouldn't put anything past either of them. Word from my nephews is that he's livid over Casey's legal actions to bring him to justice and to revoke the remainder of his lease on the place. Harrison claims he swore to make her wish she'd never been born."

"Well, word among the cowpunchers tending his cattle on Casey's place is that Big Joe was due to be discharged from the hospital today. His oldest son, Spencer, is transporting his butt home as we speak."

"Did you find out any additional information from Andi? I had the distinct impression that she was lying by omission."

"Yeah. It seems Ben didn't think it was a good idea for them to fill either of us in about the sheriff stopping Casey. He must have thought we would pick up where we left off on our initial contact with Tucker."

JD hadn't been in the old house where he grew up very often since the death of his dad. Ben's parents had kept the place in good repair while he was half a world away disrupting other people's homes. Ben took care of things at the ranch that was once again home for Cassie.

He was more exhausted than he'd wanted Rick to know. After opening some windows to get a feeble breeze circulating, he stretched out across his old bed. It felt strange. These days, he was used to sleeping in the huge old bed that had belonged to his dad and mom. However, the bed and a few other well-worn treasures from the days when he was a sane person were over at the other ranch he owned a piece of. He sure hoped Cassie wouldn't trash them in a pique over his abandonment of their promising relationship.

It was a brief encounter in the rain on the lawn of her grandmother's home that floated around in his beleaguered mind as the curtain of sleep closed around him.

He spent the next week working on the old place and chopping some firewood for the coming winter. Rick or Ben stopped by on a regular basis to keep him apprised of the goings-on at the other place. Ben dropped the tidbit that he rode Cassie's Appaloosa when she went on her daily ride and Andi was off somewhere with Rick.

"That's an interesting development that he neglected to mention in his reports."

Ben chuckled. "Yep…I think the big guy is smitten. He's been a little down since he and Casey drove her to the airport."

"Is he okay with staying on at the ranch now that she is gone?"

"Oh, yeah. He has a soft spot for Casey and has bumped me on occasion to ride with her."

"Rick is riding a horse?"

"Don't sound so shocked. After all, you told him not to let her out of his sight. But the first time was pretty comical, and I had to listen to all the complaining about sore muscles that he didn't even know existed."

"I really don't like the idea of Cassie being alone while we're in court next week."

Chapter 14

Casey was already missing Andi, even though she'd spent more time with Rick during her last eight days. Still, it had been nice to have an old friend and another woman around. She was finally caught up on her work and decided to lavish some attention on her equine companions. She snagged a couple of apples from the fridge on her way out. It was early evening when she entered the barn to groom her charges. Bucky took his grooming as his due and showed little emotion, but Chief loved his back and belly being massaged with the curry. He bent his body like he was made of rubber. Then he placed his muzzle on an itchy spot on his side if he wanted a more vigorous application of the currycomb in that location. He stretched his neck out and curled up his lip when she curried the designated spot. Chief always lightened her funks and made her laugh.

Casey didn't laugh much at all anymore, not since Gram's passing. The utter rejection by JD added to her complete lack of humor. She really appreciated her delightful rescue horse. He seemed to be on a mission to return the favor. His blue roan coat was smooth as silk and glistened as a result of his improved health and care. The nasty wound to his chest from a trailer accident had healed over fairly well. Much to Casey's delight, Chief was able to recover enough to be one heck of a good riding horse. The scar had ended his show career and put him on a one-way path to an auction. Casey had ended up in a bidding contest with a few killer buyers. It amazed her that he was so willing to hop into a trailer. She gave him an affectionate pat on his spotted, snow-capped hip blanket, and returned him to his stall.

A blazing orange sun was low on the horizon and sinking into the distant mountains when she started back to the house. The early August heat seemed unrelenting. A cool shower would be a slice of heaven. She had the eerie feeling that someone was watching her, and she scanned the porch on the ranch house. Rick was seated in one of the chairs, boots propped on the railing, chugging on a beer. He glanced over her shoulder. She turned to see what caught his attention and was shocked to see her recurring dream come to life. Again she walked toward him. He stood on high ground, backlit by the sun, and was only a silhouette. She knew how this ended, but was still drawn to him.

Casey proceeded slowly, like a sleepwalker, moving up the slight rise to reach out to him. It was obvious he was tall with broad shoulders, but he appeared to be pathetically thin. His hair was nearly shoulder length. Just before she could get close enough for a good inspection, he placed his hands in his pockets once more, bowed his head, backed away from her, and turned to retreat. He faded into the setting sun and the thickening darkness exactly like the nightshade that he was.

Tears ran down her face as she stomped her foot on the ground like a frustrated child. She thought his face looked bearded as he turned away from her. She did not recall that from any of the sketches from her nightmares. "You son of a bitch," she whispered into the dark. Then she remembered the large, ominous shadow that always separated them in her dreams; she scanned the immediate area for the threatening entity, but found it absent. She walked back down the hill, intending to question Rick about the strange visitor. He was no longer on the porch, and unsure how much brew he'd guzzled, she decided to table the discussion. Instead, she thumbed through the sketches that she'd been hastily sketching over the past three years, but they didn't shed any light on the strange visitor. It struck her that since her arrival at her early childhood home she'd not experienced that haunting dream. Was she losing her mind and now suffering hallucinations? She was about to call it a night when she got a call from Bob Jackson reminding her of the court date for Rick, Ben, and JD the following morning.

"Do you want me to send a car for you, Casey?"

"No, I'll ride in with Rick."

"See you tomorrow, then."

Casey hung up the phone, wishing she could merely not show up. However, Bob managed to convince her that it would agitate the three men who needed to be on their best behavior should she remain at the ranch. She wasn't particularly concerned about Ben, but the other two were on short fuses; she didn't want to be responsible for either of them ending up in prison. It was the consensus of the male contingent, according to Bob, that she was somehow to blame for their assault on the lawmen.

As Casey piled into the pickup early the next morning, she noticed that Rick didn't look as if he'd managed any sleep either.

"Good morning," she greeted him.

He grunted.

"Well, so much for pleasantries." She decided to wait a few minutes to see if he would respond. Since this was going to be one of his crappy mood days, she didn't see any reason to beat around the bush. "Did you see the man at the top of the hill last night?"

"Yeah."

Great! I just love one-word conversations, she thought. At least he saw him, too. "Do you know who it was?"

"No. He didn't appear armed or to pose a threat. If he had, I would have handled it."

Casey guessed that eliminated Rick as the threatening shadow figure. She made a conscious effort to purge the incident and similarity to her dreams from her mind. She needed to be clear-headed for the ordeal ahead. She'd not seen JD since their altercation in the rehab room at the VA hospital. Her gut clenched. Her nagging stomach and an unrelenting headache were not good indicators for the rest of the day. Every muscle in her body was taught as a bowstring. The uncontrollable urge to reach over and smack Rick upside his head had taken hold of her. Smacking him might relieve some of her tension, but would be a really dumb move. The thought flitted through her mind that if he punched out her lights, she wouldn't have to worry about making it through the trial.

******

Courtrooms were somber places that to Casey felt much like funeral parlors. The same sense of loss, pain, and grieving permeated every surface, nook, and cranny of the room. Her taciturn chauffeur for the day was the first of the defendants to arrive. Bob Jackson greeted them before escorting her to a gallery seat directly behind the defense table, equipped with four chairs waiting for those being prosecuted.

She was aware Bob had tried for a change of venue, asserting that Big Joe held undue influence in the county. Casey didn't doubt the accusation one bit, but he probably had just as much clout throughout the state. She glanced over at the prosecutor's table and noted that Big Joe and the pot-bellied sheriff were in deep consultation. The entry of Ben and JD shifted her attention.

Casey thought that she was prepared to see JD again, but she would not have recognized him if he'd passed her on the walk outside. He was gaunt and pale to the point that his blue eyes stood out in stark relief on his bearded face. Wisps of gray accented his nearly black, wavy hair, which flirted with his shirt collar, and he had a slight hitch in his gait. His gaze swept her as he approached his designated seat. She was positive she saw a fleeting grin as he took in her garb. She'd opted for a clean pair of jeans, a light blue camisole top, a blue embroidered jean jacket, and black western boots. Maybe what he thought humorous was the fact that he was dressed similarly. Unlike his co-defendants, he'd refused to wear the suit and tie recommended by their attorney. He strode in wearing rough-out boots, Levis, a light blue western-cut shirt open at the collar, and a denim sports jacket.

Could JD have been the shadowy visitor of last evening? Casey's speculation of JD as the long-haired, bearded man of the night before was interrupted when the judge entered the room. Once everyone was seated again, she was amazed at the number of people who'd filed in while she was concentrating on the defendants. It was easy to spot the journalists, but the others were open for speculation. One marine and two naval officers had taken seats in her row. Casey wondered why they were present.

Casey scanned each face on the jury. Four women were scattered among what looked like a couple of accountant/banker types, and the other six looked like blue-collar guys of varying ages. Two of that group looked old enough to be retired or close to it. Oh well…so much for their right to a trial by a jury of their peers. That thought registered as she listened to the opening remarks of the prosecutor.

"The state will prove that the three defendants assaulted officers of the law in the performance of their duties." He pontificated for another twenty minutes before Bob Jackson addressed the jury.

Assistant District Attorney Roth began his case by putting Sheriff Tucker on the stand that afternoon, following a lengthy lunch break.

"Sheriff, what was the reason for your visit to the Hoffman Ranch on the evening of June third, two thousand and nine?"

"I was investigating a shooting on the highway earlier that afternoon, which resulted in a traffic accident that hospitalized Mr. Joseph Gannon and his driver."

"Why would you assume James Donovan Gannon or anyone else would have any involvement with the shooting?"

"Mr. Joseph Gannon made a statement at the hospital that the most likely suspects were JD and his co-owner of the ranch, Cassandra Hoffman."

"At that point, what did you do?'

"I obtained a search warrant for all the buildings on the Hoffman place."

"What were you looking for?"

"I'd hoped to find a rifle capable of making the shot that blew the tire on the limo."

"And did you find it?"

"No. Before I mounted the stairs to the back porch, the big blond guy—I think his name is Rick—went into the house."

"Sheriff Tucker, do you see this person in the courtroom?"

He pointed an accusing finger at Rick. "He's the blond one at the defense table."

"Let the record show that the sheriff has identified the defendant Rick O'Bannon. Continue, Sheriff."

"I figured he was stashing the rifle, if it was there. I told JD, who was still seated on the porch, why I was there and that I had a warrant to search the place. That's when he attacked me!"

Once more, Roth had the sheriff point out the person who attacked him to make sure the jury had a complete picture of events. "Then what happened?"

"Deputy Smith took a position on one end of the porch, and Deputy Hickman took the other. Rick showed up again and disarmed Smith while I was grappling with JD, who'd gone for my gun. The Mex kid took Hickman's handgun."

Roth finished with the sheriff, and Bob Jackson picked up the cross-examination.

"Sheriff Tucker, are you in the habit of arriving in force to question an upstanding member of this county?"

"JD is unstable and dangerous. I was being cautious."

"Did you know from personal experience that JD was dangerous?"

"No. I didn't have personal experience with him, but I heard he'd gone around the bend since he got home from a VA hospital back east."

"Okay, let me get this straight: you arrive with the preconceived notion that there was going to be a confrontation, so you arrived with backup and in an aggressive posture. Is that correct, Sheriff Tucker?"

"Yes."

"Thank you, Sheriff. No more questions, Your Honor."

Roth called Deputy Smith next, and by the time Bob Jackson finished his cross exam, Rick was the hero of the debacle. Smith admitted that Rick O'Bannon had diffused the situation and then escorted the deputies around the property while they searched.

Hickman told the court that he, like Rick, had tried to calm things down by handing over his handgun to Ben, who hadn't been the least threatening. It looked like the prosecutor's whole case rested on Sheriff Tucker's claim that JD had attacked him.

Roth asked for a continuance until the following morning. The groans were audible. Rick and Casey went back to the ranch to check on the place and feed the horses. After chores they were to meet the rest of the group for dinner and a briefing for the following day.

True to style, Bob had secured a private dining room for the meeting and a meal. Thankfully, he put off the courtroom strategy until the waiter cleared their dinner plates. Coffee carafes and water pitchers were placed on the long conference table instead of the customary after-dinner drinks.

"The charges of assault against Ben and Rick will most likely be dismissed. I'll make that motion tomorrow. That leaves JD."

The plan was to put Ben and Rick on the stand to give their version of events.

"JD, our best strategy is to mount a defense based on events and the character references that I have lined up. I don't want you on the stand where you would be subject to cross-examination by Roth. He would try to provoke you, which would hurt your chances for acquittal."

"That could prove to be a problem. No matter how it's told, I did go after Billy Tucker and disarmed him."

"We can't dispute that, but we can show the sheriff was there to provoke a confrontation."

JD objected to Bob's plan to put Casey on the witness stand.

"She wasn't there. What's the point of involving her?"

"It goes to the unwarranted aggression on the part of the sheriff."

JD left the room with Ben in his wake before Casey could approach him about the previous night. She was sure that her shadow man was JD and that he had cut his hair and trimmed his beard for the morning court appearance. Had her shadow man been JD all along, and not her father, as she'd begun to believe?

She and Rick left the briefing twenty minutes behind the others after conferring with Bob on the following day's proceedings. They discussed Roth's move for a continuance.

They'd been on the road toward home close to an hour when Rick broke the silence.

"Are you okay with taking the stand, Casey?"

"I don't know. It's a new experience."

******

Casey was thunderstruck upon entering the courtroom the following morning. There, at the defense table, sat Andi. She was so preoccupied conversing with Bob that she didn't notice Casey and Rick until he took his seat.

Casey chose the same seat as the previous day and resumed her people watching. Less than thirty minutes later, Andi was seated to her right directly behind the defendants, and the military trio was on her left. The reason for the continuance soon became evident. Roth called Mr. Joseph Gannon.

"Mr. Gannon, the defense has tried to paint Sheriff Tucker's investigation of the persons of interest in the attack on you as being over-zealous. Could you shed some light on why the sheriff would think he needed backup to question the occupants of the Hoffman place?"

"The sheriff indicated his intent to question the co-owners of the ranch, and I told him not to go there alone."

"Why did you warn him?"

"I stopped by to welcome JD home when he first returned to Colorado, and I was met at the door by O'Bannon, who threatened to blow my head off if I set foot on the twenty acres that surrounded the house."

"Were you able to see JD on that occasion?"

"No, but I could hear him."

"And what did he say?"

"He said 'just shoot the son of a bitch, Rick, and do the world a favor.' He barked it out like an officer issuing orders."

"So you had good reason to suspect that JD or Rick may have made an attempt on your life?"

"Yes."

"Why did you name Cassandra Hoffman as a possible suspect?"

"She took an instant dislike to me, and after she started fooling around with JD, she sided with him. She's also initiated court proceedings to remove the lease her father had given me on all the property except the twenty acres immediately surrounding the house."

"Did she threaten you?"

"No, but JD did, if I didn't back off with her."

"Thank you, Mr. Gannon."

Bob Jackson was deliberately slow in approaching the witness for the cross.

"Mr. Gannon, is it not true that you are better known as Big Joe Gannon and that you prefer to be addressed in that manner?"

"Yes."

"On the day of the alleged shooting that resulted in the traffic accident that hospitalized you and your driver, did you see a shooter?"

"No."

"Yet you made accusations against JD Gannon and Cassandra Hoffman?"

"Yes."

"Did Miss Hoffman ever threaten your life?"

"Not directly, but JD did in regards to her."

"I remind you that you're under oath. Please answer yes or no. I repeat, did Miss Hoffman ever threaten your life?"

"No."

"So, according to your testimony, the only person on the Hoffman Ranch to threaten to blow your head off was Rick O'Bannon. Is that correct?"

"Yes."

"Then why was Sergeant Rick O'Bannon not named as one of your suspects?"

"I was in pain and had a concussion. I must have forgotten about O'Bannon."

"Isn't true that you've been receiving death threats for years?"

"Yes."

"Yet when you saw an opportunity to extend your vendettas against your brother, JD, and Cassandra Hoffman, you sent the sheriff in to instigate a confrontation."

Roth jumped up to object.

"I withdraw the question, Your Honor."

The judge excused Big Joe and asked the prosecution for additional witnesses. The prosecution rested the state's case. Defense would begin following a two-hour lunch break.

Casey was still trying to wrap her head around the fact that Bob had known the last-minute witness for the prosecution was Big Joe. Their attorney thought Roth had unwittingly handed them a gift. Big Joe's antipathy toward JD was readily apparent to even a casual observer.

Andi's presence was a backup for Casey, should her recollection of events break down to a "he said, she said" confrontation between her and the sheriff. Rick couldn't be happier with the turn of events. He hadn't stopped grinning since early morning when Andi made an appearance.

None of them ate much. Casey didn't know about the others, but her stomach was tied in knots, and she was grateful that Ben and Rick were up first.

Ben Ramirez was sworn in, and he led off the case for the defense.

Bob started off using Ben's surname to establish a respectful tone with the jury. Most of the blatantly anti-Hispanic jury candidates had been challenged and dismissed during the selection process, but you never could be sure of a person's prejudices.

"Mr. Ramirez, take us back to the evening of the sheriff's official call. What were you doing at the time?"

"We were kicking back, watching the sunset, enjoying a beer, and talking about the odd day we'd had. Little did we know that it was about to get a whole lot more unusual. Two vehicles came tearing up the long drive from the direction of the County Road. We identified them as Sheriff's units when they got closer."

"What did you, Rick, and JD do?"

"We didn't do anything. We continued to sit on the porch, sipping our brews of choice. The closer the three law officers got, the more obvious it was from their attitude that they'd come to pick a fight. That scared the hell out of me."

"Were you intimidated by the attitude of the sheriff and his deputies?"

"I might have been if I'd been alone. However, I was more concerned about my two companions, who'd spent multiple tours in war zones. They would not take well to a show of force by anyone."

"At what point did you feel that things got out of hand?"

"Rick went into the house to relieve himself and was challenged by Sheriff Tucker. Rick more or less told the Sheriff to try to stop him. Fortunately, Tucker didn't respond to the challenge. Instead, he turned his attention to JD. Not one of us missed the flanking move by the deputies. I was amazed that JD sat there without moving a muscle while just staring down the other man."

"Had Sheriff Tucker explained his purpose for the unexpected visit?"

"Oh, yeah. He told JD that Big Joe had been shot and that he was a prime suspect. He also said he had a search warrant for the ranch."

"And what was JD's reaction?"

"He didn't appear to me to be paying much attention. It wasn't until the Sheriff included Casey as suspect that JD grabbed the front of his uniform and pushed him against the porch support. His threatening tone when naming Casey as a suspect was the catalyst for the whole assault debacle."

"Thank you, Mr. Ramirez."

Roth was champing at the bit. "Mr. Ramirez, in your testimony you stated that you three were drinking on the night in question. Is that correct?"

"No. Rick and I had a couple of beers. JD was drinking coffee."

"Do you expect this jury to believe that while the two of you were swilling beer JD was teetotaling?"

"He was drinking coffee."

"Did the sheriff actually threaten Miss Hoffman?"

"It was more his tone than actual words."

"Let's try this with a simple yes or no. Did Sheriff Tucker threaten Miss Hoffman?"

"Yes."

"Mr. Ramirez, are you an American Citizen?"

"Yes!"

"Then you understand the penalties for perjury."

"Yes."

"I ask you one more time. Did Sheriff Tucker threaten Miss Hoffman?"

"If I can only answer yes or no, then the answer is yes."

"Your Honor, would you instruct this person to answer my questions without the colorful commentary?"

"Mr. Roth, the witness has answered your question twice, and need I remind you that on the testimony of the deputies, Mr. Ramirez and Mr. O'Bannon's charges have been dismissed. Do you have more questions for this witness?"

"No, Your Honor."

"Mr. Ramirez, you are excused. Mr. Jackson, call your next witness."

Rick was sworn in.

"Mr. O'Bannon, would you tell us why you left the back porch to enter the house when the sheriff arrived?"

"It was obvious to me that the deputies were trying to flank us while Sheriff Tucker made a frontal assault. I moved to keep all three of us from being trapped in a crossfire."

"Where did you go?"

"Back out the front door. Then I worked my way up the side of the house to come up behind one of the deputies. That's when JD bolted out of his chair and grabbed Sheriff Tucker by the front of his uniform."

"What happened then, Mr. O'Bannon?"

"We disarmed the officers, put their firearms in the back of their vehicles, and then I escorted them while they searched the place."

Roth started his cross-examination by maligning Rick's character. "Mr. O'Bannon, is it true that you and JD Gannon have been brothers in arms for many years?"

"Yes."

"Is it also true that September of 2007, you faced a military court for the murder of an American private contractor?"

"No."

"You are under oath, Mr. O'Bannon."

"I killed the back-shooting son of a bitch, but I didn't murder him."

"According to the transcript, you claimed that the person was targeting Captain JD Gannon. Is that accurate?"

"Yes."

"Isn't the reason you left your home in Illinois and now stay at the Hoffman Ranch, so you could continue to protect your former captain?"

"I needed a change, and JD offered me a home."

The rest of the morning was spent with the JAG officers and the marine who'd occupied the seats at the end of the row where Casey watched the proceedings. In effect, they were character references for the decorated military defendants. Rick had been cleared of all charges and honorably discharged. JD was released for medical reasons. Casey was put on the stand after the lunch break too attest to the hostility of the sheriff and the fact that he didn't bother to inform her that the residents of her ranch were occupying the jail.

It only took the jury three hours to come up with a not guilty verdict on the charge of JD assaulting the sheriff. The jury must have bought the testimony of the military contingent that if JD had attacked Sheriff Tucker, he wouldn't be here to tell the story.

Hostility radiated from two of those gathered around the prosecutor's table. Casey wasn't the only one who noticed the visual daggers flung in their direction.

Rick's eyes pierced those of Big Joe, issuing an unspoken challenge and threat of his own. Casey had a bad feeling that they hadn't seen the last of JD's malevolent half-brother.

Chapter 15

"Are you nuts?" was what came out of Casey's mouth, though her mind was listing a multitude of objections to Andi's announcement that she and Rick were going to wed.

"I love him."

"Good Lord. You barely know him."

"When it's right, its right. I knew it the first time we met, and neither of us want to be apart."

Casey shook her head as she turned to retrieve a cup of hot chocolate from the microwave. She sure hoped that her impulsive friend knew what she was doing. Rick was a handsome devil, but he tended to have massive mood swings. She wondered if he were bipolar or suffered from some form of PTSD. The doctors and counselors at the VA told her when she'd visited JD there were milder forms of the disorder that plagued him. She also learned that PTSD didn't always show up immediately. An unknown trigger could bring it on years down the road.

Casey sat at the kitchen table after placing a hot mug in front of her friend. "What is the rush? Don't you want a church wedding with your family and friends around you?"

Andi's cheeks turned a bright pink. "I really don't want to wait that long to be Rick's wife."

"How soon are you planning the trip to Vegas?"

"Rick is checking on flight information; I won't know until he and JD return."

Casey was feeling queasy, but she wasn't sure if it was the thought of flying or the fact that JD would be going along. She hadn't seen him for at least two weeks, since he'd left the courtroom without so much as a glance in her direction. She tried to beg off of the maid of honor role, but Andi's emotional meltdown had Casey acquiescing. She wondered if Rick had also coerced JD into being his best man? JD had made it clear that he didn't want to be anywhere near her, but now they would be paired up for their friends' wedding.

"Why don't we go shopping? I could use a new dress for the occasion."

"Great! I need a wedding gown, too."

Andi did a little online search of likely dress shops in the area, and they were on their way before noon.

Andi struck gold at the third bridal shop they visited. She found a satin, designer, A-line wedding gown with a beaded pop-over jacket that fit her to perfection. The bride to be who had originally ordered the creation had canceled, thereby losing her deposit. Andi went home with the gown for less than half of the original price. "I need to find shoes after you find a dress."

"You could probably go barefoot and not a soul would know."

"Real funny, Casey. I am not going to let the gown brush along the floor and muck up the hem and small train. Don't you think my bare feet would ruin the elegant overall look?"

"Well…if you're going for elegant, I guess shoes are a must."

Casey ended up with a pale green, full-length, satin dress. It was a one-shoulder design with a diagonal neckline that plunged under her left arm. The satin hugged her curves to midway between her hip and knee, where it flared into soft folds to the top of the matching open-toed pumps. Andi went for a pair of higher heels in white satin.

They were waiting to check out their shoe purchases when Andi's phone started whinnying. Rick and JD had returned to find both of them missing. Andi appeared flustered and began making apologies for not letting Rick know where she was. Casey grabbed the phone.

"Look, O'Bannon, we're almost finished here, but we're not coming back yet. We are going to the Steak House for dinner. You're welcome to join us or fend for yourself. Oh, yeah…we might take in a movie afterward. Bye." She ended the call and handed the phone back to Andi.

"God! Casey, what did you just do?" Her friend had articulated every word as if she were talking to someone with very little understanding of the English language, and Andi was sure Rick would take exception to her tone.

"You might as well find out what you're dealing with before you're tied down with someone you have to get permission from to take a pee!"

"He's not like that. It's only worry over this Big Joe threat."

Casey held her opinion of the Big Joe situation to herself and paid for their shoes.

They got waylaid at the jewelry store looking at earrings, and by the time they arrived at the Steak House, Rick was already there. He had JD in tow, and it was hard to say which had the most threatening scowl. JD didn't speak a word, but his disapproving stare spoke volumes. Rick was more vocal. "Where the hell have the two of you been?"

His attitude sucked for a potential dinner companion. For once in her life, Andi was tongue-tied, so Casey took him to task. "We were shopping."

"I thought you said you were winding it up when I talked to you." He glanced at his watch. "That was nearly two hours ago!"

"Well...a couple of the stores kind of sucked us in."

"Did it ever occur to you to call us?"

"No."

"What the fuck do you mean, no?" His voice had gone threatening and rumbled from deep within his chest.

"I don't have to account to you or anyone else for how I spend my time. If you plan to growl at us all through dinner, Andi and I can find another place to eat."

As if on cue, the hostess escorted them back to a table. Rick latched on to Andi's arm and all but dragged her through the dining room.

"Cripes, he's reverting to caveman tactics," Casey mumbled, and noticed a devilish grin spread across JD's bearded face.

Once the orders were placed, Casey went on the offensive. "So did you get seats on a flight to Vegas?"

"We have tickets for a three forty-five flight on Friday afternoon."

"Stop frowning at me, Rick. Did you make room reservations?"

"JD took care of that chore."

Casey stiffened her spine and put her question to JD. "Are there more rooms available?"

"I can check. What do you have in mind?"

"We have almost forty-eight hours until our flight. Plenty of time to get plane tickets from Hopkins or the Akron Canton airport for Andi's family."

"Casey, my folks can't afford plane tickets and hotel accommodations."

"Don't you want them to come to your wedding?"

"Yeah, but."

"No buts. It's my wedding gift to you. What about you, Grumpy, is there someone that you would like to be there?" Rick didn't answer; he merely shook his head in the negative.

They paired up following dinner. JD was riding shotgun in her little red Yukon.

Casey couldn't get over how different he seemed from the man who had hijacked that seat on the trip to Central Ohio where she purchased Bucky. That memory felt like an event that happened to them in another lifetime. It occurred to her they were as strangers, but the silence was not the uncomfortable type. She kept her attention on the road even when she felt his intense blue eyes scan her form. She felt unexplainable heat wherever they landed!

******

Casey thought she had everything under control. She and JD had managed to secure a block of rooms on the level below the bridal suite reserved for Rick and Andi following the nuptials. Andi's brother, Andrew, and his wife were coming, as well as her mom and step-dad. Bonnie and her current love interest were arriving on the same flight as the others.

She was busy doing some research on her laptop and trying to ignore the constant jolt to her system every time she brushed so much as an arm against the male in the seat next to her. Her attraction to JD rankled, he'd turned his back on her, and she had enough abandonment in her life not to want to risk rejection ever again. Her thoughts had strayed, and she'd evidently been staring at the display on the screen an inordinate amount of time. She gave herself a mental shake when he spoke to her.

"Is there a reason you're looking at kitchen designs?"

"I want to remodel the kitchen in the old house. Its outdated and dysfunctional."

He hoped that meant she was thinking of staying in Colorado. Then she burst his small bubble of hope. "Selling the place would be extremely difficult without updating it," she informed him and switched to another floor plan.

"You just got here. Why don't you give it a chance, Cassie?"

"I guess I'm stuck here for a while. This is a major project. Did you have the wiring updated when you did the other renovations?"

"The contractors that I brought in wired the first level everywhere except the immediate kitchen area. Ben was supervising the renovations and told them to wait until one of us made a decision about what to do with it."

"Well, perhaps you and Ben can contact that company or person when we return to see if they are available to tackle the job." She turned the power off on her Mac, closed her eyes, and tried for some down time to recharge her own batteries.

JD gave Casey a gentle nudge on the shoulder to wake her. She opened her eyes, blinked, and smiled at him. He figured she must be caught in the fog that comes from being disrupted from a deep slumber. She'd never smiled at him since her arrival at the ranch. He cleared his throat before speaking. "Better buckle up. We're on approach." He knew when she focused on her surroundings and came back to reality: her cold, stoic demeanor replaced the warm smile that had sent his heart rate up and constricted his airway. She didn't reply or speak to him again until they arrived at the hotel and were checking in.

"Andi will stay in my room tonight. I guess that puts Rick with you."

JD merely nodded his head. He and Rick accompanied the women to the fourth floor. Rick gave Andi a tongue-thrusting kiss that left her knees wobbling. "JD made dinner reservations for this evening after your family checks in. Get some rest." He winked at her and kissed her once more. "You sure won't get much sleep tomorrow night."

Casey swiped the key card and held the door open for her friend and the young man with the baggage cart. She tipped the hotel employee while she continued to prop the door open with her back. "Ah…um! Can't this wait until later or tomorrow night?"

Andi turned a bright shade of pink, but Rick shot back with a barb of his own. "We could make this a double wedding, Casey. I'm sure JD would be agreeable. Then you would be too occupied to worry about us." Casey held up a middle finger salute. Rick laughed. "Exactly!" She grabbed Andi by the arm, dragged her into the room, and slammed the door in his laughing face. A frustrated growl escaped from deep in her chest as she locked and bolted the door.

******

"Why the hell don't you just ask her?

"Back off, Rick. Throwing my own words back at me isn't going to change my reluctance to make that move."

"I was uneasy about taking the plunge, too. Do you think you're the only one of us who has trouble leaving all the war crap behind?"

"Does Andi know that?"

"We talked about it some. And she told me Casey took it on herself to warn her that PTSD could turn up years down the road. It looks like she did her homework all the months she spent making the trip to Virginia to spend time with you while you were going through rehab."

The discussion continued between the friends and longtime comrades-in-arms while they waited for the arrival of Andi's family. Of the two, JD was suffering more anxiety about the pending wedding and the social gathering.

Back down the hall, Casey had given up trying to calm Andi down. After a not-so-subtle suggestion that her friend take a cold shower, Casey plugged in her earbuds, selected her favorite tunes, and stretched out on the double bed closest to the window with the drawn drapes. She blocked out the world and tried to rest before the stress of dealing with the best man.

Chapter 16

Casey was suffering from an excess of partying. Her head felt like a balloon ready to burst, her stomach rolled as if she was in a ship on a stormy sea, and her eyelids were stuck shut. She finally managed to pry open small slits for her eyes to peek through. Something wasn't right! Her eyes popped open and she rolled over to take in the room. The sudden move caused an intense bout of vertigo that had her groaning and grabbing the side of the bed for stabilization. "What the hell?" she croaked out.

The hotel room was backward. It was the mirror image of what she remembered. The same desert tan walls with white trim. The same rust, tan, and green geometric pattern was on the window drapes and the spreads of the two double beds, one of which was still made up and undisturbed. That kind of made sense to her since Andi was now married and residing several floors above in the bridal suite. Then she realized the shower was running in the bathroom.

She put her feet on the floor and slowly stood while balancing on the brass headboard. At that point she became aware she was wearing a man's white dress shirt! "Oh, crap!" she whispered into the darkened room. She gathered her crumpled dress and under things, and then made her way to the door when the shower turned silent. Casey quickly disengaged the door chain and lock.

Safely back in her own room, she kicked of her shoes, rid herself of the male shirt that fortunately had covered her to her knees, and stepped into the shower. She felt cleaner but not much better than when she had awakened in the strange room. The lifesaving ibuprofen was easy to locate in her small traveling case. Casey downed two with a tall glass of sickly warm tap water, and collapsed across the bed wearing only a mint-green terrycloth robe.

The phone jolted her back to consciousness, and she fumbled with the receiver of the house phone. "What?"

"Casey we're all waiting for you in the dining room."

"Why?"

"Because you set up a reception dinner for this evening for the bride and groom."

"Bonnie, what time is it?"

"It's almost six. I've been trying to call you for over an hour. Where's your cell phone?"

"I'll be right down, as soon as I change."

"Is it too much to hope that JD is with you?"

"Why would JD be with me?"

"You left together, and he isn't here yet either."

Casey set a record dressing. She slipped into a yellow sundress, shrugged into a white bolero jacket, stepped into a flat pair of white sandals, and dumped the contents of her dress clutch into a white shoulder bag. Her hair was tied back with a yellow scrunchie and she was checking out the overall effect in the wall-length mirror on the bathroom door when the door began to groan with the beating it was getting.

She yanked open the door, and there was JD decked out very similarly to his first day of the bogus court case. He was scowling at her as he handed her cell phone to her. "That thing has been going off for the last three hours."

She took it from him and put it on the charger, and then left with him to join the others.

They took a bit of razzing for arriving later than the newlyweds, but all in all, the spur of the moment reception went off with out a hitch. Casey drank only iced tea and water with her meal. She didn't want any repeat of last night. It wasn't that she was embarrassed about what had happened after leaving the party; it was that she couldn't even remember what had happened or how she got to be in JD's room.

The pastry chef did a magnificent job of creating a three-tiered wedding cake decked out in white and yellow roses. The new Mr. and Mrs. Rick O'Bannon disappeared following the cake cutting. Andi's mom was charged with taking home the top layer with the bride and groom riding on top. Andi's family, along with Bonnie and her very distinguished veterinarian companion Harlan Lynch were booked on an early morning flight to Cleveland. Things began to break up shortly after Rick and Andi left the scene.

JD had booked an afternoon flight for their return to Denver to give them time to tie up any loose ends. Over breakfast, Casey broached the subject of the hours that remained missing in her memory of the night of their friend's wedding. "Okay, JD. How did I end up in your room after we all finished casino hopping the other night?"

"You had a few too many drinks. You danced with everyone that came for the wedding, and half of the men at each stop. Water would have been a safer choice to quench your thirst, but you seemed to be enjoying yourself. So I just kept an eye on you."

"Did I dance with you?"

"Only once. That was all that I could handle."

"Did your hip cause you pain?"

JD chuckled and gave her an evil grin. "No. It wasn't my hip, but a slightly lower part of my body that was causing me extreme discomfort from holding you close after such a long time."

"Okay, but that still doesn't explain how I ended up in your room that night."

"You said that you didn't want to be alone."

"I said that?" Boy, she thought, that was absolutely out of character. "And I just hopped into bed with you?"

"No. After you complained about not having anything to sleep in, I gave you a shirt out of my closet. Then you fell face first onto the bed. I woke up when you crawled under the covers with me."

"Then what?"

"Then we slept the remainder of the night. I got up to shower, and when I returned you were gone. I found your cell on the floor later when it started playing its little musical notes for me. The tune is haunting. What is it?"

"Are you going to tell me that you didn't take sexual advantage of the situation?" His deep blue eyes turned glacial, and she felt like sparks were going to shoot from them any second.

"I've never forced myself on a woman in my entire life, and I'm too damned old to change my ways." He threw some dollar bills onto the table and got up to leave.

"Open up your heart and let the sun shine in."

He looked down at her upturned face. "What?"

"That's the song my grandmother used to sing to me when I was cranky or out of sorts as a child. It's the ringtone on my cell, now."

He reached out his hand to her. "We need to check out and settle up."

Casey took his hand and walked with him as far as her room. She packed her things including the borrowed shirt. She planned to wash and press it before she returned it to him.

They rode the shuttle to the airport in companionable silence. On the flight to Denver, Casey researched some additional kitchen plans and bookmarked three that she liked the most. JD promised to give her the number of the contractor he'd hired for the restorations already completed when they got back home. Casey didn't correct his use of the word "home" although she still intended to sell the ranch. There was no sense, in her opinion, in shattering their fragile truce. She was tired of all the hostility, and she still had hopes of bringing Big Joe to justice.

There was a bite in the air when they landed in Denver, and the frost on the windows of her Yukon required a bit of scraping and the use of defrosters while the engine warmed. Casey was wondering if it was this cold at the ranch and considered the advisability of blanketing her horses.

Ben had just finished feeding her equine friends, and the barn was her first stop. The unloading of her luggage could wait.

"How are my beautiful boys?" They both twitched their ears and nickered at her. She fished in her pocket for the two peppermints she taken from the bowl on the desk of the hotel restaurant that morning and unwrapped one for each of them. By the time she bid them a goodnight and returned to the Yukon, JD and Ben had unloaded her luggage and placed it in the hall of her new little house.

The weather was cold one minute with snow, but by afternoon Casey was often shedding her coat. The same held true with the horses. She'd always tried to keep their coats down during the winter so they wouldn't get their long winter hair wet with sweat when she rode them. Mid-October brought some unexpected changes in their lives.

Rick and Andi were expecting a new family member in the spring. Andi was still working as a paralegal, and Rick had taken a job with a private security agency. They were living in Andi's condo while it was offered on the real estate market.

Either Ben or JD rode with her on her daily outing, and Casey drove JD to his appointment with his doctors at the VA. Rick was no longer in residence, so that left the escort up to either Ben or Casey. JD agreed to her driving only because he didn't want her home alone. Casey found out JD never drove off of his ranch or the one they shared. He admitted to her on one of their trips that he saw snipers and IEDs at times, and it wasn't safe for others for him to operate a vehicle on the highway.

Casey was caught up on her work, so she decided to start clearing out the kitchen cabinets and the pantry of the ranch. She kept a few antique glass pieces and an old tea service that she found, but packed up most of the stuff to donate to Goodwill or some other worthy local group. Neither Ben nor JD would let her give away the cast iron pots.

She climbed up the three-step kitchen stool and onto the counter to reach the very top shelves of the old cabinets, and found that they were exceptionally deep. Her finger barely touched what felt like another old cookbook. JD walked in and nearly scared the life out of her. "What are you trying to do, break your neck?"

"Stop yelling at me and see if you can reach the book at the back of this shelf." He put his hands around her waist to lift her from the countertop. He stood on the second step and retrieved the book, and then handed it to her.

She glanced at it and thumbed through the pages as she had with several others she had found, but this one was different. It was handwritten, and Casey suddenly realized she had found a link to her mother. The book hidden on the top shelf in the old kitchen cabinets was her mom's journal. Casey held the precious leather bound book to her chest and wept.

"Cassie, what is it? Are you okay?"

All she could do was nod her head. Casey turned to exit the back door, but halted before stepping onto the back porch to look back at him. "This kitchen is a disaster. You can have dinner with me until we get things squared away over here. Give me thirty minutes to get cleaned up, then bring your appetite."

Casey had placed her precious volume on the nightstand beside her bed where it rested while she showered. She set the table for two, and JD was right on time. She grinned at his fresh out of the shower look and his apparel. Once he removed his jacket, she could see that he had opted for a heavy flannel shirt of dark green to complement his snug-fitting jeans. Quite often, their choice of outerwear would be similar, as if they had tried to coordinate the look. He must have been thinking the same thought as he scanned her jean-clad form; she was wearing a dark green sweatshirt of nearly the same shade as his shirt.

She was slicing a loaf of French bread when she asked, "Do you prefer coffee or tea with your dinner?"

"Whatever you have."

"I made a pot of tea, but it would only take a few minutes to brew some coffee."

"Tea is fine."

The only time she could remember him having a cup of tea was seated at this table when he visited them at Gram's house over three years ago. She put a filter and grounds into the coffee maker and added water. While it dripped into the glass receptacle, she dished up the beef stew that had been cooking in the crockpot while she was busy trashing the kitchen in the other house.

Casey placed a heavy mug at his place and served him a large bowl of stew. She returned to the counter to retrieve the hot coffee, and then filled his mug before filling her own with tea.

JD waited for her to be seated before he began to eat. It was the best beef stew he'd ever tasted. "This is delicious!"

She laughed. "You sound surprised that I can cook."

He placed his fork in the bowl and frowned as he looked into her eyes. "That isn't how I meant it."

"I know. Relax and eat. Actually, my grandmother taught me how to make it. The secret is to let it slow cook throughout the day."

He ate a second bowl of stew and two slices of apple pie. Casey thought trashing the other kitchen could end up being a good thing. She had a hunch he didn't eat well now that he was alone in the house. Maybe he would gain some weight. She wondered if Rick had been the designated chef. She could understand; it took her a long time after she lost Gram to begin to cook for herself. She still had to force it sometimes. She didn't like to eat alone, either. He helped her with clean-up and the dishes. She seldom used the dishwasher for the few dirty dishes and utensils one or two people created. Casey washed and directed the placement of the items as JD dried them.

After JD left, she curled up on her bed to begin reading the written account of her mom's life.

The journal began with...

Kathryn Joan Curtis-Hoffman - Book 3
Colorado
June 15, 1977 -

Casey placed the book gently back on the nightstand, and then rose to lock down the house. She set an unopened box of tissues beside the book; she was going to need them to plug the leaks raining down her face. She decided reading her mom's final entries was going to be more difficult than she'd thought. The lack of an end date on the first page undid her. She heated a fresh mug of tea and wished that she had something to spike it with.

She changed into her ratty old sweatshirt that she preferred to sleep in when the weather was cold and scooted under the bedclothes. She settled into the pillows that she'd propped against the headboard, took another swig of tea, and picked up the dark leather book with the age-yellowed pages.

June 15, 1977

Bill met a man at one of the water conservation seminars he'd conducted, a few months back, who had a small ranch for sale. I only found out about our new home on April first, and I thought that he was just joking with me. I've been nagging him to find us a house. Things are a bit crowded with the two boys and all their toys in our small apartment. I bought this new diary at a drug store in Omaha while picking up some snacks, drinks, and more baby aspirin. I thought that the move to a ranch and the new chapter in our lives deserved a fresh journal.

Casey turned out the small reading light on the nightstand where her mother's words also rested for the night. Her last thought before exhaustion claimed her was the location of her mom's earlier diaries.

The next morning, she prepped the coffee maker, turned it on, and went to feed the horses. She'd taken on the morning feeding so Ben didn't have to arrive as early. JD was already in the barn filling water buckets, and the horses were busy munching hay.

"Did you already grain the boys, too?"

"No, I didn't get that far."

Casey got the grain ration for her equine friends and added a scoop of vitamin supplement to Chief's ration. "Eat up, guys, we'll go for a ride after we have our breakfast." She turned to JD. "Coffee is hot, and so are the muffins. I'll start the eggs. Come up when you're finished." He merely nodded and gave her a strange sidelong glance.

He showed up as she was dishing up a healthy portion of scrambled eggs and bacon onto his plate. "Sit," she ordered, like he was a kid or a puppy in training. He was scowling at her. "What's wrong? Don't you like your eggs scrambled?"

"Scrambled is fine. I'm just not used to being ordered around."

She laughed as she filled his coffee mug. "Sorry. I'll try to remember to say 'sit, please' or 'please sit down' from now on."

He drank some of the coffee and snagged a blueberry muffin to add to his plate. He looked over her smaller portion of eggs with only two slices of bacon. "Are you trying to fatten me up or something?"

"Trust me, you could use a few more pounds. I don't think you've been eating properly."

"I'm not one of your rescue critters, like the old spotted horse in the barn."

"Chief isn't all that old. My vet said he was about ten. He was badly hurt, half starved, and consigned to an auction frequented by meat buyers."

"Am I supposed to ride him this morning?"

"If you want to."

"Yeah, well…it's not a matter of want to, but you're not riding off alone."

"Don't you ride?'

"I used to when I was young and before the artificial hip."

"You can have your pick, but Chief is a much smoother ride than Bucky. Even Rick didn't bounce around much on him, though he did heap a bunch of expletives on your head."

JD had to laugh at the mental picture of his old friend trying to navigate the horse. Now, he was married to a horsewoman. Life sure takes some bizarre twists and turns, he thought.

******

Nearly a week had passed since Casey found her mother's journal. She continued to make meals for JD while emptying the kitchen in the ranch house. She worked on her computer in the evening hours before retiring to read a bit more about her family prior to her birth. She was methodically reading through her mom's accounting of events a day or two at a time to prolong the sense of connection with her lost family.

Mom had mentioned meeting young Jimmy Gannon a few weeks after arriving at the ranch. Everyone, including his mother, Val, called the child JD. It seemed she called her husband Jimmy, which Casey's mom found amusing, for the senior James Gannon could easily have been his wife's father. Mom had a feeling that there was bad blood between James and his elder son, Joe. Joe's wife and children showed up for the Independence Day Bar-B-Q that the Hoffman family had been invited to. The children all got along well and had a lot of fun. Mom enjoyed the warm reception from both Val and Melinda Gannon. After that picnic, Casey's mom felt better about the isolation of the ranch.

James and Val dropped by a couple of times a week whenever Bill returned to Kansas or was in the field. The couple always brought JD with them, and he struck up a friendship with Casey's brother Bill. Things progressed much that way through the remainder of their first summer at the ranch. Her dad was away for extended periods of time leaving, her mom to cope with the two boys and the ranch.

Casey was preoccupied with thoughts of what her mom's life must have been like and almost tumbled from her step-stool when JD walked in. He moved quickly to steady her.

"Sorry. I didn't mean to startle you."

"It's okay. You kept me from crashing. I need to quit anyway and make us some lunch."

"Why don't you let me buy lunch while we're in Denver?"

"Why are we going to Denver?" She didn't remember a planned trip for today.

"Carter just called. He had a cancellation and can sit with us to discuss the kitchen project around four. Gives us plenty of time to have lunch."

"Are you sure about this? I know you don't like the heavy traffic or the city."

"I'll be fine. You can drive, and when we get to Denver you can hold my hand to keep me grounded." He gave her a devilish grin.

"Don't push it, JD."

He only laughed at her threatening tone.

Casey was relieved that JD handled the trip in without any incidents. Maybe he was improving. Perhaps Rick's absence in his daily routine was a good thing. He rode with her every morning now, and Chief nickered enthusiastically whenever JD entered the barn.

Lunch went well and so did the trip over to CS Remodeling. The place was small—about twice the size of her leased studio back in Ohio. It had great lighting and the walls were lined with samples of building materials, as well as a nice selection of cabinets and countertops.

JD introduced her to Carter Smith, and Casey got right down to business.

"Mr. Smith, I've narrowed my selections down to three possibilities, which I think would be a good place to begin. One thing has changed since I chose these plans. I would like to save the original cupboards and incorporate them into the plans if that is possible."

Casey saw JD raise a questioning brow. She hadn't discussed this aspect with him.

Carter took a look at her plans and the photos stored on her laptop. "I would like a copy of these to refer to as we progress." Cased pulled a small flash drive from the same large bag from which the computer had materialized. "Excellent, Miss Hoffman. Let's take a look at some countertops."

Carter penciled in an appointment for the following week to look at the existing cabinets that Casey wanted to save. On the way back to her vehicle, JD broke his silence. "I didn't think you cared about saving any of the old kitchen. I thought the idea was to simply update it so the house was more marketable?"

She glanced over at him. He sounded too hopeful for her comfort. "That's still my focus, but the existing cupboards are hardwood, and if I'm not mistaken, are made of oak. It would be a shame to have to destroy them." He didn't utter a word, merely nodded his head in reply and focused on the road as they pulled out of the drive. Casey decided to try for some conversation to relieve the building tension. "JD, do you know where I can pick up a couple of steaks for our dinner before we get out of town?"

"There's a freezer full of them back at the ranch."

"I don't remember any steaks in the freezer at the ranch."

"I was talking about my place. Not the Hoffman ranch."

Wow. She realized his mood had made a big about-face. She tried again. "I'll have to remember that the next time we do steaks for dinner. You can bring them, but it would be better if we could find some not frozen ones for tonight's dinner."

He pulled a small cell phone from his jacket pocket, flipped it open, and punched a name in the directory much harder than necessary. Casey kept her eyes on the traffic and the road ahead, but she heard every word and voice infliction as he spoke. "Ben, we're on our way back from Denver, but the traffic is still heavy. Would you feed the horses? Thanks. Do me a favor and snag a couple of nice sized steaks from the freezer before you leave, and pick one out for yourself if you haven't had dinner. Just set them on the kitchen table in the ranch house." He placed the phone back his pocket. "There, the steaks should be thawed by the time we get back."

There was an overturned tractor-trailer that backed up the bumper to bumper mess even more, and it was dark when they arrived back at the ranch. JD hadn't uttered a sound since the few terse words he'd spat at her following his conversation with Ben. He exited the Yukon and went straight to the back door of the ranch house.

Casey didn't know how to deal with him, so she didn't even try. She opted to enter the house where she started the coffee, put on the teakettle, and headed for the shower.

JD lingered over a third cup of coffee after Ben had left for home. His presence eased the tension as they filled him in about the meeting with Carter. "I'm sorry, Casey. I guess the whole trip didn't go as well as I'd hoped, but that was no excuse for my behavior toward you."

"Well, most of the day went off without a hitch. It was a lot longer day than we had anticipated, and maybe we tackled a bit more than you were ready for. Are you okay, now?"

"That's a loaded question. I guess the meds were wearing off. I took them when we got back, so I'm relatively docile at the moment."

Casey doubted there was such a thing as a docile JD Gannon, but she thought that it was possible he needed the illusion. She really needed to bone up on the PTSD thing and the side effects of the medications he was taking.

Chapter 17

The holiday season was fast approaching, and it had been a difficult time for Casey since the loss of her grandmother a few days following Thanksgiving of 2006. She decided to bake for the holiday and send Christmas care packages to Andi and Rick, Bonnie, and Ben and his mom and dad. She wasn't sure what to do about the Thanksgiving Day meal, so on their morning ride a few weeks before turkey day, she broached the subject with her riding companion.

"JD, what do you usually do for Thanksgiving?"

He looked at her in a strange manner. "They usually served turkey, stuffing, and some other slop, topped off with a slice of pumpkin pie at the mess hall wherever I was stationed."

"What about after that?"

"Last year we were invited to have dinner with Ben and his parents, Hector and Rosa."

"Did you go?"

"Yeah. Rick hauled my butt over. I was pretty uncomfortable, but it went pretty well."

"Why were you uncomfortable? Aren't they old friends?"

"I wasn't the same person they'd known, and I wasn't sure what they expected of me. Also, I didn't trust myself.

They were putting the horses away when Casey resumed their previous conversation. "Do you think that they will be expecting you again this year?"

He shrugged his shoulders and threw some hay to the horses.

"I could make dinner here, and you could invite them this year if you want."

"I'd rather it was only you and me, but it would be a nice gesture. Let me run it by Ben. He has a pretty good handle on his mom's idiosyncrasies, and I'll let you know in a couple of days. But be forewarned, Rosa is an incorrigible matchmaker. She's been trying to foist her female relatives and daughters of her friends on me for nearly two decades. Ben says she is constantly interrogating him since she found out you came back home."

"If Rosa's so curious about me, why hasn't she just stopped by?"

"She doesn't drive, and Ben won't bring her. He told her that you weren't ready yet and would pack up and go back to Ohio if pressured."

"Great! What a bunch of male morons!" She threw her hands up in the air and stomped back to the house, mumbling to herself the whole way.

Over breakfast the following morning, Casey took matters into her own hands. "I'm going to visit Rosa today."

Her jaw was set. and her eyes were flashing when she made her announcement. JD thought she was looking for an argument. "Do you know where she lives?"

"You said that Ben and his parents lived on your ranch, so I Googled it."

"Are planning to drive over to the ranch?"

"What do you think? I'm sure not walking over there."

"I think we should take our morning ride in that direction and kill two birds, so to speak."

Casey thought Ben was going to fall over when they rode up to the little white frame ranch complete with a surrounding white picket fence. He recouped quickly and took Bucky and Chief over to a large pole-barn. His mother was at the door, and she opened it with a huge smile plastered on her face.

Rosa was a few inches shorter than Casey and twice her girth, with an ample bosom. She looked like the female version of Ben. They possessed the same dark eyes, coal black hair and engaging smile. She was not what Casey had expected. Not a speck of grey showed near her temples or in the long ponytail that hung below her shoulders. She was garbed in denims with frayed bottoms, and a maroon sweater.

Ben's exuberant mom enveloped JD in a huge bear hug and kissed him on his cheek as he leaned down to return her hug. She was in the midst of scolding him for not coming around more often when he interrupted her to introduce his companion. Then, it was Casey's turn to have the breath squeezed out of her. She wondered if everyone but her had been brought up in touchy-feely families; Andi's folks were like that, as was the Portland Hoffman clan. Now it appeared that Ben's family was also among the group that made a habit of invading personal space.

"I was wondering when I was going to meet you, Casey. Please, sit at the table. Would you like some coffee?"

Casey took the offered seat, but JD excused himself to check on the horses and give Ben a hand with chores. Rosa placed a hot mug of coffee in front of Casey and sat down to join her.

Casey wasn't sure how to begin. "Have you known JD for a long time?"

"I've known JD most of his life. I cooked and kept house for Mr. Jim after his wife passed. JD was only six, the spring he lost his mother. I think of him as one of mine."

"Did you know my parents, too?"

"I did. You look like your mother."

"I've heard that. Rosa, I wanted to invite you and your family to Thanksgiving with us this year."

"You mean at the Hoffman ranch, with you and JD?" She sounded shocked.

"Yes."

"Does that mean that you're going to stay?"

"Well…until spring, at least. It will take that long to whip the place into shape, so that it's marketable."

"I accept, on the condition that you and JD join us here for dinner on Christmas Day."

"That sounds like a plan!"

Over another cup of coffee they discussed the menu and what Rosa wanted to contribute to the turkey day feast.

****

Casey was too busy with baking before and after the Thanksgiving Day dinner to resume the nightly ritual of reading her mother's journal. When not baking or shopping, she was ferrying packages loaded with baked goods to the closest UPS outlet. Andi's package included a couple of cute little onesies and a bib. She couldn't resist the baby clothes decorated with little horses. To add to the holiday madness, she suddenly had three new prospective clients. She was busy putting marketing packages together for CS Remodeling and the small countertop manufacturer that Carter had referred to her after seeing her portfolio. Both businesses were looking to start a new marketing campaign the first of the year. Bob Jackson also referred a client who was opening a second real estate office in the Denver area.

By March, Casey had locked down the new account with CS, and another with the manufacturer who supplied countertops for his remodeling jobs. Carter had taken down the existing cabinets. They now resided in his workshop where they were being stripped and would be stained to match the new additions that would be used for the island with a butcher-block top. His crew was removing walls and rewiring the kitchen.

JD was having trouble with the invasion of the workers, and Casey didn't think the plaster dust was good for him, so she suggested he move in to the guest room at her place because he flat refused to leave her alone and move back to his ranch for the duration.

With everything progressing on the kitchen front and her new accounts purring along, Casey resumed the nightly reading of her mother's journal. There wasn't much after the accounting of her family's first Thanksgiving and Christmas at the ranch.

April 25, 1978

My heart is breaking for Jim Gannon and little JD. Val lost her baby and her life three days ago. Jim is coping with the aftermath and funeral arrangements. JD is with us, and he is most welcome. I thought it strange that his family didn't step up, until Melinda stopped by to see JD. Over a cup of tea she told me that her husband, she calls him Big Joe, constantly made nasty remarks about Val following her marriage to his father. He often called her a gold digging whore, and JD a little bastard who could have belonged to anyone including him. Melinda's sons would repeat his slurs. Spencer lost his temper and repeated what he'd heard to JD, who promptly punched his lights out and broke his nose.

Fate takes strange twists and turns. Val and Melinda became friends. Melinda confided, to me, she was seriously thinking of taking her sons and returning to her family in Virginia. He was abusive with her and the boys when he was drinking. Melinda had asked Val what Big Joe had against her, and Val told her. "Our family was new to Eastern Colorado when I first met Joe. We dated a few times, but he was pressuring me to do things that I didn't want to do. I went out with another guy from over near Pueblo. Joe and a couple of his friends followed us. They beat Carl senseless. Then Joe raped me and told his friends that they could have sloppy seconds. I was still a virgin when he took me, but he told the police that he'd been with me a lot of times, and I never objected before."

Melinda wiped her tears with a tissue and told me the assault on Val took place in 1970. Her parents turned their backs on her. Jim Gannon took her in and healed her body and soul. They wed before Christmas of that year, and JD was born August of '72. There is no substance to my husband's accusations.

JD can stay with us as long as he and Jim need. I've only met Big Joe a couple of times. He always gave me the creeps. Now, I know why.

Casey had a hunch that JD didn't know how far back Big Joe's animosity toward him started. His hatred went all the way back to Val's rejection of him and her marriage to their father. She put the journal on the nightstand and went to make a hot cup of tea. She spiked it with the brandy she's purchased on her last run for provisions.

She was sitting in the semi-darkness with only a nightlight in the wall plug over the counter lighting her tearstained face when he walked in. "Are you drinking?"

"A little brandy in my tea helps me sleep."

"Is there any left?"

"You mean tea or the brandy?" She sniffed, wiped her eyes and blew her nose.

He took note of the pile of tissues beside the floral printed Kleenex box sitting next to the bottle of brandy. "Actually, I was referring to the tea. I don't drink anymore."

"There should be a couple of cups left. Help yourself."

She watched him fix a cup, add a bit of sugar, and sit in the chair opposite her. His hair was rumpled, but his blue T-shirt was unwrinkled, and his jeans were zipped but not fastened. She figured he quickly donned them on to see why she was prowling the house at three in the morning.

"Do you want to talk about it?"

"About what?"

"Why you're out here in the middle of the night putting a dent in that bottle of brandy and the box of tissues."

She thought about what had upset her, but she couldn't share that with him. "I don't know if I can explain it. I was reading some of my mother's diary and suddenly felt a strange sense of loss. She was so out of her element and my dad was away more than he was home. At the point where I quit for the night, she'd lost one of the two friends she'd made here."

He looked into her tearstained face. "My mom?"

"Did you know they were friends?"

"Not at the time. I was pretty young, and you know how kids are they live in a world of their own. They really never think of their parents as having friends or a social life, but it makes sense that they would be friends. Maybe, you should put the journal away in a safe place and not read it for a while."

"I haven't read it since before Thanksgiving, and picked it up again a couple of nights ago. The last was just a sad entry." She rose and refilled her teacup and topped it off with a splash of brandy. She noted the disapproving scowl on his brow. "I'm sorry that I woke you."

185

JD rinsed out his cup and placed it in the plastic dish drainer. What he wanted to do was wrap her in his arms and carry her back to his bed where he could hold her for the rest of the night, but he kept his distance. "Goodnight, Cassie."

After cleaning up the mess from her meltdown, she also retired for the remainder of the night. The brandy worked wonders, and she was sound asleep as soon as her head hit the pillow.

A heavy rain kept them from their morning ride. Casey did a little housecleaning while JD fed and did the barn chores. She put on a pot of soup to simmer for their lunch. She pulled the sheets off both beds and threw them into the washer. After lunch, she worked on the presentation for a new antique outlet opening back in central Ohio. It was too early to start dinner, so she curled up on the couch and opened the diary to where she left of the night before. The next entry was in June.

June 15, 1978

JD left us last week to return home. Jim finally found a cook and housekeeper who he liked. Her name is Rosa Ortez. JD seems to like her, and I think she will give him some of the warmth and caring that a young child needs. He tries to put on a brave front, but I know he is hurting.

We go over a couple of times a week so the boys can spend time together. Bill's parents sent us a twenty-one by forty foot above ground pool. The delivery people set it up and a huge water truck emptied its contents to fill it. Now, I have to read all the literature to figure out how to operate it and keep the water clean and safe for the kids. Fortunately, Bill's parents included a half dozen child-size life vests, a couple of boogie boards, a pool version of a basketball, and a floating hoop.

Melinda and I organized a picnic and pool party for the kids next Wednesday. I invited JD and Rosa to join us. It is to be a fun day for the moms and kids.

Casey didn't remember anything about her childhood on the ranch and wondered if the pool still existed when she came along and whether she had played in it too. JD entered so she closed the journal. He looked aggravated.

"Cassie, have you been over to the ranch house today?"

"No. The guys were complaining to Carter that I was breathing down their necks."

"Yeah. Well, maybe, you need to be. Put some shoes on and come with me."

The beautiful slate tile at the entry to the family room was littered with old wall studs. Nails still protruded from where they had been tied into the header and footer framework. Plaster remnants from the pantry were strewn throughout the dining room. Muddy boot tracks mingled with the plaster dust and tracked down the hardwood floor to the half bath in between the office and the family room. The sink was filthy and the toilet un-flushed. Casey spun around and ran back to the other house to retrieve her phone.

She took photos of the mess, including the hole punched through the wall between what was the pantry and the dining room. That wall was to remain intact. She looked at JD, "Anything else? What about the bedroom and the master bath?"

"I didn't get that far." The walked down the hall, through the bedroom and into the blue and grey tiled bath. "Doesn't look like they messed with anything in here."

"Yeah. They knew this was your space and didn't have a death wish. This mess was deliberate. I don't get it. What changed? They were so careful up to this point. They were even using plastic tarps up to contain the plaster dust. Come on, JD, let's get out of here."

Back in her home office, Casey uploaded the photos to her e-mail. Then she placed a call to Carter Smith. He answered on the second ring. "Carter, are you still in your office?"

"Probably be here for a couple of hours yet. Is there something I can do for you?"

"You bet! You can fire the crew that was here today. I'm sending you some photos I just took. Check your e-mail and then call me back." She ended the connection and e-mailed him the cause for her irritation.

He called back within ten minutes. "Casey, I'm on my way."

Casey threw together some spaghetti, using a store bought jar of sauce, a salad, and placed a few hard rolls in the breadbasket on the table. They ate in silence. Both were preoccupied with dark thoughts and trying to control their equally volatile tempers.

They were working on the after dinner clean-up when Carter arrived. They met him in the drive and escorted him to the ranch remodeling disaster.

"Jesus! I've never seen anything like this. It looks like deliberate sabotage."

"That's what we thought."

Carter took a video of the mess. Before they all went back to the other house for a conference, Casey made another pot of coffee while she listened to Carter talk to JD.

"I'll make this right, JD. A crew will be over in the morning to clean the construction mess up, and when they're finished, I'll send in a cleaning team."

Casey put in her two cents. "NO!" She set a mug of coffee in front of each man.

"What are you objecting to, Casey?" Carter thought he was being more than fair in trying to salvage the disaster,

"The construction crew clean-up is fine, but I don't want anymore strangers in that house. I'll clean it myself."

"The cleaning people we use are licensed and bonded, Casey,"

"So were the men doing the work on the tear out and look how that turned out. What happened to the original crew?"

"The job foreman got a better offer from somewhere and quit. Two of the others came down with the flu. I was short-handed and hired a couple of new guys to complete the removal of the wall between the kitchen and the pantry. They had references and were previously bonded, so I hired them and had them bonded. They worked on finishing up a couple of jobs, and I thought they would work out for finishing up this one."

JD looked him square in the eyes. "Don't you think it strange that your foreman on this project gets hired away, and the others turn up sick?"

"I didn't think much of it at the time, but now that you mention it the whole thing is kind of fishy."

"Do you know my brother, Big Joe?"

"You can't operate around here without knowing who Big Joe is."

"Has he ever lent you money?"

"No. But I wouldn't swear to the same about some of the suppliers I use. Do you think he had something to do with this?"

"I wouldn't put it past him. He wants this place and he has only a little over two years left on the grazing rights that Cassie's dad gave him. He's done far worse things to further his land holdings and to wreak havoc on those who thwart him."

"I'll file a vandalism report with the sheriff's office in the morning, and fire the crew first thing."

Casey gave Carter a sidelong glance. "That's probably a good business move to file a report with law enforcement. It will most likely help with insurance claims and such, but I wouldn't mention our discussion about Big Joe's involvement. Sheriff Tucker is bought and paid for by Big Joe, and it could cause you some serious retaliation."

Casey sat at the kitchen table waiting for the tea to brew with her head bowed and resting on her crossed arms. She raised her head slightly to peek at JD, who was now sitting across from her with a mug filled with the last of the coffee. "Do you think that Carter owes a debt of some sort to Big Joe?"

He watched her scoot her chair back and retrieve a mug that matched his from the overhead cabinet while he mulled over her question. "I think he is a victim in the trashing at the ranch house, as much as we are. He's just more collateral damage in Big Joe's feud with me."

She splashed a heavy dose of brandy in her mug before taking her previous position at the table. "His feud with *us*!" she emphasized as she took a swig of the bracing brew. Then she set the mug on the table. "Do you remember anything about the Hiram Stokes incident? I know Bob updated you on some of the events."

"I remember he said you were being followed. When the police arrested him, they found out there was a hit out on me."

Casey took a few more gulps of the hot brew; it seared on its way down her throat. "When I realized that someone was stalking me and went to the police, they found a tracking device on the Yukon. It was placed there before I got back from my trip to Denver for the reading my dad's will."

He must have sent Stokes that night after he dropped me at the airport or first thing the following morning."

"JD, it occurred to me while we were talking to Carter that perhaps none of the suppliers had a hand in what happened. What if Big Joe had someone plant a bug in the house?" She was almost whispering, and she had turned her DVD player to an earsplitting pitch. She moved to a seat closer to him. She continued her train of thought. "There were a lot of people in and around here lately: the crew that erected this house, the movers who delivered my things, and the contractors working on the kitchen in the other house. Anyone of them could have been paid to plant a listening device."

JD considered what she was speculating, but he had a different take. "I agree with the possibility of a planted bug or two, but I don't think that he would hire someone he couldn't control. More likely, Sheriff Billy Tucker did it. He would have had plenty of time to come back here while Rick and Ben were locked up, and I was in the damned VA."

"You know, JD, that makes a lot of sense. At the time he stopped us on our way here, I thought he was only mouthing off. He said, 'I'll be keeping an eye on you, along with the rest of the inhabitants on your place.' Then he never came back around and we didn't see him until we went to court. Is there a way of locating those kind of devices?"

He didn't say a word, but nodded his head.

"JD, if he has been listening to everything going on around here, then he knows about our finding my mom's hidden journal."

"Is that something that should worry him?"

"I don't know. I'm just getting into her first mention of him. I need to finish the diary, and then find a safe place for it."

June 30, 1978,

Bill came home from the seminar on water conservation with a new local pal. Of all the people in Colorado Bill had cultivated a friendship with Big Joe Gannon during a lunch break and then dinner following the event.

Melinda extended an invitation to our family on behalf of her husband for a Fourth of July picnic and fireworks. The way she talked, I felt that she was hoping we wouldn't accept, so I told her that we had plans to spend the day together and make a special day for the children.

However, Bill took it on himself and accepted Big Joe's invitation to our family. I didn't want to go and we had a big fight. He said that I didn't have to go, but he was taking the boys. I'm not letting my children go there without me.

July 6, 1978

What a nightmare. I could feel Big Joe's eyes tracking me the whole afternoon and evening. I was so grateful that Jim and Rose brought JD late in the day so that he could see the fireworks. Billy and Carson were delighted that their friend had joined them for the evening. I sought some quiet time visiting with Jim and Rosa. I thought it was particularly telling that Jim never joined the group of other men who congregated around Big Joe. Then I remembered that his elder son hadn't been there last year when the Independence Day shindig was held at Jim's place. Only Melinda and her sons had attended when Val was still alive.

The boys returned to sit with us during the fireworks. Bill finally tore himself away from his new friend to converse with Jim, and spend some time with his family. Carson fell asleep in my lap halfway through the fireworks. Billy and JD were wound up and enjoying the light show in the night sky. I overheard Jim warn my pigheaded husband not to get too chummy with Big Joe, and that he needed to protect his family. Then Jim told Bill that his elder son couldn't be trusted. I felt a chill run up my spine.

Bill and I got into another big argument. I informed him that when he returned to a full teaching schedule at Kansas in August, I was going home to Ohio. I told him I was going to look for a place near my folks for the boys and myself. He went into a full rant about how I was the one who wanted a larger place for the boys to grow up. He stormed out when I told him all I wanted was a house with a yard and a swing set, not ranch in the middle of nowhere.

July 20, 1978

Rosa and I put together a party for little Billy's seventh birthday. I'd called Melinda to invite Spencer and Harrison, but hadn't heard back from her. We had cake, ice cream, hot dogs, and soda. I had let Billy pick the menu. Rosa made a taco salad, which was a real hit with adults and children alike. My fruit salad and veggie plate was pretty much ignored by the kids. Bill still hadn't showed up when the kids were served the cake and ice cream. Billy opened his gifts with the enthusiasm that only a child is capable of. He opened the package from Carson and me and smiled from ear to ear at the huge paint-by-number boxed set. Next he went for an even bigger box from JD and Jim. He needed Jim's help to lift it onto the picnic table. Once the wrapping was torn off, he let out a loud whoop! He got a duplicate to the Erector Set that belonged to JD. The two boys spent hours at Jim's home playing with the set. He was about to open the last of his packages when his dad drove in with a horse trailer dragging behind his blue Cherokee. Big Joe's bright red Eldorado trailed behind.

Bill unloaded a black and white pony decked out with a big red ribbon. Billy was thrilled with his new hay burner. Big Joe brought Spencer and Harrison, but there was no sign of Melinda. Big Joe gave Billy a saddle and a red pad for beneath it; the matching bridle was supposedly from Spencer and Harrison.

The party fizzled at that point. Jim took JD and Rosa home. I put a sleepy Carson down for a nap and started clearing up the mess left behind. Bill complained about removing the food when he and his friends hadn't eaten yet. I excused myself to check on Carson and told Bill that he knew how to work the grill.

We went another round that night. I don't know who he is any more.

August 24, 1978

Bill left for Kansas last week. We are still here only because today is JD's birthday and the boys and I were invited. Like our son Billy, JD has reached age seven. Melinda and her sons were a no-show, but there were loads of kids at the party. Jim had invited all the little kids who belonged to the ranch hands on his place. 'No gifts' was written on the invitations along with the suggestion to only bring a smile and have a good time. And all the kids had a marvelous time. That is what a kid's party should be.

August 29, 1978

The kids and I are packed. I bought a Suburban and splurged to have it outfitted with a tow package. Pokey is loaded along with his tack and feed. I called Bill this morning to tell him we were leaving the ranch. He told me that he would talk it over with me later. It seemed he was late for class. I'll just bet that if his new buddy Big Joe called, he would make time.

The boys were very good and so was Pokey. We stopped in Iowa for the night at a place that could accommodate our pony. We should be able to make it to the boarding stable near Mom and Dad's house. They think the boys and I are coming for a visit. I don't want to put them in the middle of our dispute.

September 10, 1978

I found a temporary accounting job that has the potential to be permanent. Billy is enrolled in kindergarten and Mom is watching Carson. We're staying in the upstairs bedroom that used to be mine when I was living at home. Pokey is boarded over on Mastic Road, and they have plenty of room to leave the trailer parked there. Bill still hasn't contacted me, and I wonder if he is under the misconception that we are still at the ranch waiting for him. I had to come clean with Mom and Dad when I registered Billy for school.

Casey laughed out loud. Her mom wasn't the sweet, mild-mannered paragon who Gram had espoused. Kathryn had a spine and wasn't going to be a doormat for anyone! She'd reached her limit and rebelled. Casey yawned, turned out the lights, and placed the precious book on the nightstand next to her bed. She'd locked up before crawling into her bed, but she left the foyer light on for JD. He had his own key.

******

She woke to snarling dogs and screams. At first she thought it was a nightmare, but then JD's voice penetrated her sleep-fogged mind. She grabbed a robe, slipped into her running shoes, and snagged her old ball-bat from the closet of her room. Then she opened the door and ran toward the fray.

Two large Shepherd-looking dogs had one man down near the propane tank at the rear of her home. He was the screamer and was pretty well chewed up. He was making a valiant effort to protect his face and throat. There was another man at JD's feet. He wasn't moving a muscle.

"JD, is he dead?"

"That's usually the result when you break someone's neck."

His statement was so calm and matter-of-fact that it unnerved her. "You killed him?"

"Well, he didn't break his own neck, but he did make the mistake of drawing a gun on me. So he sort of committed suicide."

"Are the dogs going to kill that one?"

"That's up to him. He can tell me who sent him, or he can deal with the dogs." He was completely dispassionate as he watched the two dogs use the hapless man as a chew toy.

She was about to ask JD what they were doing here when the sound of sirens, and the eerie red and blue strobes, disrupted her thought process. The sheriff's vehicle was roaring up the drive like he was responding to an emergency. JD looked at her and grinned. "You call the sheriff, Cassie?"

"No."

"I guess that answers the big question."

Billy Tucker jumped out of the vehicle and grabbed the shotgun. "You better drop that double gauge, Billy, if you don't want a bullet between your eyes." He dropped it like it was a hot potato. "Good decision, Billy. What are you doing here?"

He hemmed and hawed. "We got a distress call that dogs were mauling someone."

"Really? Way out here, someone complained about noisy dogs?"

The screamer was yelling at the sheriff to help him. "Call of the dogs, JD, or I'll have to shoot them."

Casey spoke up for the first time. "Are you a good enough shot, Sheriff Tucker, to take out the two dogs and not kill the man you're attempting to save? If you don't kill them with the first shot, I can guarantee that they will focus their full attention to you." She gave him an evil grin and then turned to JD. "I guess it's time to curtail their fun. Things could get real messy."

JD turned to the dogs. "Trooper and Justice, at ease." The dogs ceased their attack and came to sit on either side of JD.

Casey was impressed. Except for the blood spatter on their coats, they could be ordinary pets. Tucker was so out of his league that she almost felt sorry for him. "Sheriff, shouldn't you call for an ambulance before this guy bleeds out?"

He returned to his vehicle, making a wide berth around the shotgun still residing where he'd prudently dropped it. Casey set her bat down to retrieve the shotgun. She handed it to JD and watched him eject the shells.

Tucker looked at the other fellow's lifeless form. "What happened to him?"

The question was directed to JD, who just glared at him. Again, Casey stepped up. "The bumbling prowler was in such a hurry to flee when he was discovered that he tripped and broke his fool neck."

Tucker looked at the flat, cleared surface and asked, "And what did he trip on?"

"Sorry, I can't solve that one for you. For all I know, he could have tripped over his own feet—" She paused. "—or it could have been divine intervention."

JD and the dogs were on alert before Casey even heard the life flight helicopter. Once the helicopter left with the two intruders, the sheriff retrieved his emptied shotgun and drove off.

"Don't you think it strange that he didn't ask what they were doing here in the wee hours of the morning?" Casey made that comment as she followed JD around to the propane tank. He took a square package from beneath the tank.

"Stay. Stand guard," he told the dogs, and then turned to her. "You too. Stay put." He took the small package out approximately five hundred yards, returned to the ranch house, and came back with a scary-looking rifle with a scope. Dawn was breaking when he fired at the strange package. It blew dirt into the sky, shook the ground, and rattled more than the windows. The horses whinnied in protest, but the dogs never batted an eye. They merely watched JD for their next command.

Casey couldn't stop trembling. Someone—and she had a good idea who—had tried to blow them into the afterlife. She was on a mission now to finish her mother's diary. As far as she had read, there wasn't anything that warranted the hiding of the journal. She had the overwhelming feeling that the attempt on their lives was because of the discovery of that final volume.

Chapter 18

Trooper tagged along with JD to supervise the clean-up crew over in the ranch house. Justice kept Casey company as she cleaned up the breakfast dishes. JD had hosed down the dogs after feeding the horses. When she finished with the dishes, Casey filled a bowl with water and set it on the kitchen floor for her canine companion. Then she took the journal and a liberally spiked cup of tea into the living room to resume her reading.

October 1, 1978

Bill has returned to Kansas to finish up the term. He had finally returned home for one of his weekend visits to find the place uninhabited. He caught a flight to Cleveland, rented a car, and showed up on my parents' doorstep. Little Billy was happy to see his father, but three-year-old Carson hadn't seen enough of him since the move to Colorado to form an attachment. I refused to return until Billy's school broke for the Christmas holiday. Truthfully, I didn't want to return, but short of filing for a divorce, there isn't much choice.

Bill was looking into a teaching position at the University of Denver. I told him if he was serious and made a commitment to be home more, then the boys and I would come back.

November 15, 1978

I had to turn down the permanent job offer since we are leaving here in less than a month. I sure hope I'm not making a mistake. Billy loves school, and he is getting really good at handling Pokey. The riding lessons really stretched my budget, but they were worth it. Mom and Dad relented and let me pay rent to help with the cost of extra food required to feed three additional people.

December 13, 1978

The trip back here took three times as long as it did when we went home in August. I still can't think of this isolated ranch as home. Maybe it will feel more that way with Bill as part of our small family again. I live in hope.

December 20, 1978

Rosa and I made a Christmas shopping trip to Denver. My boys and JD were under the watchful eye of his father. Bill, and Jim had done their shopping a few days earlier. Billy was happy to be home. He and JD were more like brothers than friends, and Billy was looking forward to riding to school with JD. Rosa and I worked out an alternating car pool for after the first of the year when school picked up again.

January 5,1979,

Bill is teaching at the University of Denver, and I hope it works out for him. Billy is very happy with his new school. Why not? He and JD are seated at the same table.

January 20, 1979

Bill is coming home later and later. He smells of whiskey and is sullen. Finally, I asked him why he was drinking and not returning home. I also brought up the subject of driving all the way home from Greeley while under the influence of alcohol. That set off a big altercation. His defense was that his friends were not welcome at the ranch. As a result, he had to meet with them at a bar and grill in Denver. I was livid. Instead of coming home to his family, he was traveling the same distance or more south. I screamed at him that I never said his friends weren't welcome here.

February 14, 1979
The kids at school traded valentine cards, and Rosa made little heart-shaped sugar cookies for the kids when I dropped JD off. We stayed for a while and the boys played. They usually try to include Carson, but this afternoon he was hanging on me. He was fussy and got sick on the way home. He was running a fever. I called the children's doctor as soon as I got home, loaded the boys back in the Suburban and drove to the clinic.
I picked up a prescription on the way home.
It was late when I got back, and Bill still wasn't home.
I put the kids to bed and made myself a cup of tea.
March 10, 1979
I thought with passing of a little time that I could put the old hurt behind me, and my life would return to normal. Bill was brought home on February fourteenth by the local law enforcement. The officer asked me if Bill lived here. I should have said no, but I claimed him. I didn't claim the other one, but Bill offered the other drunk our couch to sleep it off. Big Joe collapsed on the sofa, and I piloted my weaving husband down the hall to our room. I demanded to know why Big Joe Gannon was passed out at our place instead of in his own home.
Melinda had refused to let him in the house and threatened to shoot him if he pushed the issue. The officers put him back in their vehicle. At that point Bill tolds them that Big Joe could stay at our ranch for the night.
I was too worn out to argue with my inebriated husband. I slipped under the covers and turned my back on him. Carson's crying woke me a few hours before dawn. I put on my robe over my nightgown and went upstairs to check on him. His pajamas and bed were soaked. I changed my son and his bed, and tucked him in. Then I went to the kitchen for some baby aspirin and a glass of water. I sat there with him until he fell back to sleep.

I placed the glass into the kitchen sink, and started back to our room. I was hoping to get another couple of hours of sleep. If Carson didn't improve, I would be taking him back to the clinic after I dropped Billy and JD off at school.

Big Joe was no longer on our couch, and I was about to breathe a sigh of relief, thinking that he must have gone home. I was suddenly grabbed from behind and thrown over the back of the sofa where he had been sleeping. I called for Bill, but to no avail. He held me bent over with one of his large hands. He pulled up my night clothes, and I called for Bill once more. Then he forced himself inside me. When the rutting pig was finished, he threatened to kill Bill and my boys if I told anyone. I will have to hide my written recollections for now, but someday perhaps one of my children will find this diary and know the truth. I can't help but remember the filth he spread about JD's mother. I fear that I will be subject to similar slander and Bill will side with his new pal.

Casey ran to the bathroom to be sick. She cried for her mother and wondered anew about the fatal car crash that left her without her family. She put the journal in the large bag with her laptop.

She located JD in the family room, ensconced in the old armchair that usually occupied the bedroom. It was strategically placed so he could continue to monitor the clean-up. She thought he looked tired. Casey crooked her finger at him before turning to retreat back outdoors. He followed her as she wandered off toward the crater made by the explosive device. She didn't know how to broach the subject.

She stood and looked into the pit, and then blurted, "I'm going to Denver. I didn't want to tell you where we could be overheard."

"When?"

"Immediately."

"What do you have in mind?"

"I need to see Bob Jackson."

He didn't ask any more questions, but pulled a small cell phone from the pocket of his jeans and punched in a number. "Hi, can you come over here to join our other two friends on guard duty until tomorrow? See if your cousin will join you. Come armed, I'll fill you in when you get here."

She didn't recognize the cell phone as his. "Is that a new phone?"

"It's what is known as a burner phone. Make sure to leave your phone and laptop here when we go." He keyed in another number and then flipped the phone closed. "Cassie, pack a small bag. We won't be back here for a day or two."

By the time she had showered and packed a few things in the computer bag along with the journal, Ben had arrived. A short time later, a tall dark man who resembled Ben drove up in a black GMC Acadia. His cousin looked as if he could snap Ben in two with little effort. It quickly became evident that he was the owner of Trooper and Justice.

JD filled Ben and Harlan in on the pre-dawn events. Harlan removed some equipment from his SUV before tossing JD the keys.

Casey gave JD a questioning glance. He waited until they were a quarter mile from the ranch to satisfy her curiosity. Billy Tucker or any other of Big Joe's minions wouldn't be looking for this vehicle. They checked in as James and Kathryn Curtis at a small motel on the outskirts of Denver and then drove to the opposite side of town to have dinner. JD was using cash for all transactions and warned her not to use either her debit or credit cards. He called Bob from the parking lot of the restaurant following their dinner.

He drove a circuitous route back to the motel, made a few more brief calls, then smashed the phone and threw it in a dumpster behind a pizza shop. He picked up a new one at a Best Buy and then continued his meandering trip back to the motel from there.

Casey took first dibs on the shower. She slipped into an old faded blue T-shirt and blue plaid boxers that she'd brought along for sleepwear. She intended to discuss her intentions with JD, but fell asleep before he finished his shower.

******

They ate a quick breakfast at the pancake house across from the motel before driving to their meeting with Bob. JD parked several blocks away, and they walked to the building that housed the firm's suite of offices. All of his precautions helped her to deal with their escalating peril.

Mary greeted them and ushered them right into Bob's office. "I cleared my schedule for the morning as you suggested, JD. Now, what's the emergency?"

JD related the events of the past couple of days, beginning with the sabotage of the remodeling project and ending with the attempt to blow them up. "Billy Tucker appearing out of the darkness at that time of night only confirmed our suspicions that the ranch was bugged. A friend is sweeping the place to locate all of them. We were a bit uneasy about the lack of any more harassment from either Tucker or Big Joe. Now it makes sense; they knew exactly what was going on. When Casey began emptying the cupboards in preparation for the kitchen update, she stumbled on what she thought was another cookbook. We soon discovered the book was her mother's last journal. Yesterday afternoon she finished reading it and wanted to confer with you."

Bob turned his attention to Casey. Her first question seemed off the subject. "Bob, did you look into the falsification of the DNA lab report that upholds Big Joe's claim of being my biological father?"

"I did, but I was unable to come up with any proof of intentional tampering or any paper trail as proof of bribery by Big Joe. The rest of my partners felt even if we could turn up proof, that his attorney could claim the same kind of tampering on the one you obtained in Portland."

"Does Big Joe or his attorney know of the Portland lab result?"

"No, because we decided not to file charges."

"Okay, then I want to file rape charges against Big Joe on behalf of my mother."

"Casey, the time limit is way past for that kind of action, even if you do have an accounting of events in your mom's diary."

"I know all about the statute of limitations for sexual assault in this state. However, there is no statute of limitations with DNA evidence, which we have thanks to Big Joe's manipulations. File the charges, Bob, and let's see what his attorney comes up with."

JD suggested she have Bob put the journal into his safe. Casey agreed, but wanted a copy of the pages in case Big Joe had minions in this office.

On the return trip to the ranch, they discussed the ramifications of what she had just done. Casey felt she had nothing to lose. Both were wearing targets on their backs, and their only choice was to eliminate the threat of Big Joe before he could kill them.

Chapter 19

The dogs were gone, the bugs were removed, and the mess in the house was cleaned up. It had been four days since she signed the complaint and asked Bob to file the charges. The eerie silence felt like the dead calm before an impending storm. She was restless and couldn't sleep. Maybe a stiff brandy laced cup of tea would help her calm down so that she could get some rest.

"Am I going to have to sign you up for AA?"

"Cripes, JD, you nearly scared the life out of me. Couldn't you sleep either? She got up to pour a second cup of her sleeping potion.

He didn't answer her, but opted to cross the distance between them and remove the bottle from her hand. He spun her around, enfolded her in his arms, and kissed her until Casey felt her knees weaken. Then he scooped her up and took her to bed. Neither of them got much rest for several hours. This encounter was a long time coming. Casey was astounded at the depth of feeling she experienced with JD. She hadn't missed sex over the last several years. It had never really moved her on an emotional level, nor had she ever experienced such intense and frequent orgasms.

Sleep finally found her as she snuggled up with JD and listened to his heartbeat. Her last waking thought was that their lovemaking had only been so passionate because neither of them knew how much time they had left.

Casey woke up alone. JD must be out doing the morning feed. She listened to the soft patter of raindrops on the roof and smiled as she recalled their rain dance in front of Gram's house. JD was different now than the man she'd met in the spring of 2006, but she knew this altered version much better. Casey had been battling her attraction to him ever since their shaky reunion last June.

A quick shower behind her, she was working on setting the breakfast table when JD returned. He poured a mug of coffee and took his usual chair at the table. Casey placed his plate of eggs and hash in front of him, and then set a basket of apple cinnamon muffins in the center of the table. He waited for her to sit before broaching what was on his mind.

"Are you using birth control pills, Cassie?"

She chewed her bite of muffin and made an attempt to not choke, but had to take a large swig of tea to aid in that effort. "No. Why?"

"Come on, Cassie, there could be consequences from our night together." He growled at her in the tone he'd used for many years to keep order in the ranks.

"You mean because you didn't use a condom?" She shot a challenging look into his turbulent blue eyes. "Am I going to catch some STD as a result of having sex with you?"

There were times that he wanted to strangle her, like now. "You aren't going to catch anything from me. But you could get pregnant."

"Well, you should've thought about that little snag before you carted me off to your bed. It really doesn't matter. We will most likely be pushing up daisies before long."

"You're not worried about the prospect of having my child?" She was concentrating on her scrambled eggs and had apparently dismissed him.

She cleared away the plates, refilled his mug, and finally spoke. "Do you think Harlan Ramirez would sell me Justice?"

He gave her an suspicious once-over, and tried to determine if she meant the double entendre that she'd just hurled at him. "Okay what is it you're getting at?"

"It was a simple question. I liked having Justice around and felt a lot more comfortable with her here. Is there something else going on that I'm not aware of?"

She was no one's fool, and his overreaction could have alerted her to more than he wanted her to know. "Your question caught me off guard. We were discussing the possibilities of a child as a result of our night together, and then you shift gears. If you aren't concerned about being around long enough for a possible full term pregnancy, why do you want to take on the responsibility of a dog? You already have Bucky, Chief, and me dependent on you."

"Cut the crap, JD! What's really going on?" She didn't buy for a minute that he was dependent on her. He was only trying to distract her from her question about Harlan.

"I doubt that Harlan would sell Justice, but he might part with one of her last litter of pups. I'll check with him this afternoon. Let's get our morning ride in. I'll go saddle the horses while you finish up here."

Neat escape, she thought. Her mind was going over what her exact words were that had put him on edge.

JD didn't want her to know that Harlan's wife was the daughter of the man accused of killing her family. Harlan, Tracy, and especially Pete Dugan were three in a long list of Big Joe's victims looking for justice. Melinda Victor, Big Joe's ex-wife, was another person with an ax to grind, and her new husband had a high-level CIA clearance with plenty of assets at his disposal. These were the people he had known about for a long time, but he was sure there was a legion of others who would probably do a happy dance if Big Joe were to meet his demise.

Their morning ride was cut short. Casey was frustrated with JD. He had clammed up and refused to converse with her. The only words to slip past his self-imposed silence were a few praises whispered into Chief's receptive ears.

Bob Jackson's silver Corvette was parked near the ranch house when they returned from their morning outing. Casey took both horses' reins as she dismounted. "I'll put them up, and you can deal with Bob."

JD didn't say a word. He executed an about face and headed toward the house. Casey was thankful she had her hands full with her equine pals. Leading two horses helped to curb her urge to throw a rock at his retreating form. She took much longer than necessary administering to the needs of Bucky and Chief. Unable to procrastinate any longer, she made her way to her house.

JD and Bob were seated at the kitchen table working on the muffins left over from breakfast, and washing them down with fresh coffee that JD must have made. Bob greeted her as she entered, but JD just scowled at her. He was probably ticked off because she took so long, and he had to play host. No doubt he was even required to carry on a conversation.

"Excuse me for a moment, Bob, while I clean up and change out of my barn clothes. You may as well join us for lunch." She scowled back at JD, but she was sure she wasn't even close at matching his obvious displeasure with her.

Over a quickly prepared taco salad, Bob shared the reason for the lack of response from Big Joe. "He was out of the country on business when we filed the rape charges, according to Roland Pratt.

He made a point of informing me that neither he nor his client were inclined to cut short their high-level negotiations to respond to such frivolous charges."

Casey figured this meeting out of the U.S. was more to establish an alibi when she and JD were blown to bits. "I suppose he was also out of the country when the attempt was made to snuff us in our sleep."

"It sure looks like a convenient coincidence. He must have been pretty confident the plan would succeed. I would have loved to be the fly on the wall when Tucker reported the results of the failed plot to Big Joe." Bob observed.

JD figured it was too much to hope that his evil sibling would keel over with a heart attack when he got the news. "He must be worried if he wants to negotiate with Cassie."

Casey figured she had missed some critical information while she was working off her pique at JD. "What does he want to negotiate, Bob?"

"Pratt claims that Big Joe is willing to relinquish the remainder of the lease on this place in exchange for dropping the bogus rape charges."

"He has to be kidding! There's only a little over two years left on that lease. Does he think that is equivalent to what he did to my mother?"

JD spoke directly to Casey. "Tell him that you'll think it over, Cassie."

"What! Are you out of your mind?"

"Look, if Bob tells his attorney you're willing to meet with Big Joe to negotiate terms, he'll have to return home."

"Do you really think he'll buy a turn around like that from me, JD?"

"Oh yeah. He'll figure the attempt to blow the propane tank scared you enough that you'll play his game."

Bob agreed with JD, and Casey felt they had the whole strategy worked out before she joined them. That was okay with her; she had a few aces up her sleeve as well.

"I'm going over to see Harlan tomorrow afternoon." She gave JD notice as Bob Jackson departed.

"You aren't going anywhere alone until we resolve Big Joe's war on us."

"Don't use your leftover officer command voice on me! I'll give Ben a call. Maybe he can go with me to his cousin's place."

"I'll drive over with you."

"I'm not sure that would be wise, considering the events of this day. I don't think I trust you."

"What the hell is that supposed to mean?"

"You figure it out." She turned to stomp back to the house, but turned to face him before entering. "Get cleaned up if you plan to shadow my every move. I'm not in the frame of mind to cook, and I need to get out of here. I'm going to Denver for a dinner and a night out." With that declaration, she slammed the door, shutting him out.

JD stood in the drive midway between the two houses with clenched fists as a string of cuss words echoed in his head. He let out a frustrated groan to repress the urge to shout them out loud as he mounted the steps to the ranch house. Better to shower and change over here than get close enough to lay hands on her belligerent little ass, he thought. She was definitely spoiling for a fight, and in his current mood, he was likely to give her one. Before hitting the shower, he gave Ben a call. Big Joe may have been halfway around the globe, but that didn't mean he didn't have operatives on the hunt for them. To leave the ranch unattended wouldn't be wise.

A well-known seafood place with restaurants from coast to coast was Casey's choice for dinner. She hadn't tried to engage him in conversation; perhaps she'd given up on him after her failed attempts to talk with him that morning. That was fine with him. He was able to focus on their surroundings. She never said a word when he asked the hostess to seat them beside a solid wall near the rear on the dining area. He sat with his back to the wall and had an unobstructed view of main room where they were having dinner.

Following their meal, Casey decided to go shopping! Then a movie was on the itinerary. JD had the uneasy feeling she was actually hoping that Big Joe's minions were tracking their every move. He wasn't sure what her game was. Could she be thumbing her nose at them by refusing to alter her normal activities, or was she showing them the battle was over and that a deal was in the making? He would bet on the thumbing of her nose scenario, but he wasn't going to fall into the trap of questioning her motives.

They didn't arrive home until well past midnight, and JD was exhausted. He was tense and irritable from watching for snipers or an assault. She had stood with her arms crossed, impatiently tapping her foot while he checked out the Yukon for explosive devices each time they returned to where it had been parked.

The lights were still on in the ranch. JD opted to check in with Ben before calling it a night. Casey was still up working on her computer when he arrived at what she called her place. He opened her office door after knocking twice. "Are you planning to work much longer, Cassie?" She didn't reply, but merely sat there staring at him. "Ben is staying the night and has agreed to escort you over to Harlan and Tracy's home tomorrow afternoon."

"Fine." She nodded her head for punctuation to her one word answer and then went back to tapping the keyboard. JD tried again. "Goodnight, Cassie." This time she didn't even look up. Either she was completely engrossed with what she was working on, or she was ignoring him. Maybe a little time apart tomorrow would help clear the air.

******

Casey got a late start the next morning, and it was a good thing JD was nowhere to be found. Ben accompanied her on an abbreviated version of her morning ride. They shared lunch, where they agreed to make the drive over to Harlan's around two. Ben explained by then his cousin would be finished with his morning chores and have time to show her a few potential puppies.

Twenty minutes before their scheduled departure, JD returned and promptly disappeared into the ranch house. She wondered where he'd been. It was unusual for him to take the truck and disappear for hours at a time without company. He still had bouts of disorientation and was apt to see IEDs or snipers in any piece of road litter. Casey put JD out of her mind as she and Ben bounced down the dusty drive toward the road in his beater Ford pickup. The front had probably been a light blue at one time, but the original bed had been replaced with a red box with stock panels that rattled loud enough to make conversation impossible, and for that she was grateful.

Harlan and Tracy lived on the outskirt of Brush, close enough to take advantage of the museum, restaurants, and shopping, but not hemmed in by the confines of the city. The old farmhouse was renovated and sported a new, tan vinyl siding with green trim and roof shingles. The entire place was fenced in with chain link, and "Beware of Dog" signs were strategically attached along the perimeter.

Ben opened the gate as if the warnings didn't exist. "Harlan should be around back," he said as they followed a walk that skirted the house. Another fence enclosed what looked like an obstacle course for training the dogs. It looked pretty much like an agility training setup, with the exception of attack dummies. The kennel was more recently built than the house. A completely modern pole building in the same tan and green color scheme as the home greeted them. The interior was cool as they stepped into Harlan's office.

Ben introduced Casey to Tracy, who was finishing up a phone conversation. "Okay, Dad, I'll update you later." She stepped around the black and silver desk after rising from her high-backed, black leather chair. The room was decorated in the silver and black theme, right down to the two silver-framed, leather guest chairs in front of the desk. The floor was a black and gray nature-stone type of product. Photos of dogs hung around the room, and trophies took up space on the top of the black file cabinets. Tracy gave Ben a huge hug and then reached out her manicured, turquoise nail-polished hand, which matched her tunic, to Casey. "It's so nice to finally meet you, Casey. I've heard so much about you from Ben and Aunt Rosa."

Casey thought the tall, blue-eyed blonde was a stark contrast in this family of dark eyed Hispanics. Her father, too, had appeared to have dark hair in the old news clippings that she had found in her research in the wee hours of the morning. She took the offered hand. "I hope you don't believe half of what they tell you. I'm really quite pleasant, most of the time."

Tracy laughed at her disclaimer. "Harlan is out checking on the new puppies. Adele whelped a litter this morning. I'll show you the way." Casey walked along with Tracy through the immaculate kennel. The floor was concrete, and each dog had large kennel with access to an outside run. Not knowing what she was getting into, Casey had worn her western boots and a pink printed sleeveless shirt partially covered by her denim jacket. Her boot-cut Levis were a far cry from Tracy's designer jeans. Her toes, painted to match her hands, peeked out of sandals that sparkled with bling.

"How are they doing?" Tracy asked her husband when they reached their destination.

"They all look healthy, and Adele is taking to motherhood like an old pro. She is doing great for a first time mom. Want to have a closer look, Casey?"

"Maybe when they are a little older. Mamma may not like the scent of a stranger on her new pups. They are so cute and helpless. It's hard to believe that they could grow up to be as formidable as Trooper and Justice."

Harlan was impressed with her consideration of the pups' welfare. "Adele is one of Justice's first litter, and she made her bones in the show world. Let me show you Justice's last pups."

Tracy excused herself to return to the house to start dinner, and Ben tagged along. Casey walked to the opposite side of the barn with Harlan. They went out a small door to a large, penned-in area where five puppies were busy roughhousing. Harlan whistled, and the pups stopped what they were doing and came to sit in front of him. "They are six months old now, and their attention span is improving. Four females from this litter have been sold to other breeders. I've retained Tessa here as a show string replacement for Adele. You can have your pick of the males. Would you like to see them work over some obstacles, Casey?"

"Sure!" The puppies followed them out into a runway that led to the training area. Harlan left her there with the five puppies. Two of the boys were tan with the black saddled backs like their sister

Tessa. The largest male was more silver, but was marked similarly to the others. They all looked more like Trooper than their darker mom. The fifth pup looked smaller than the rest, but his size could have been an optical illusion. He was coal black. Casey squatted down closer to their level and watched them inspect the obstacles. Tessa and her black brother came over to check her out. "Hi there. Are you ready to show off for me?" Tessa wagged her tail and let Casey pet her before she wandered back to her other brothers. The black male just sat there watching with his head cocked. "Aren't you going to say hello?" He continued to sit slightly out of reach, like he was weighing all the pros and cons.

Harlan returned with Justice, and all the pups rushed over to greet their mom, all except the black pup who stayed put and continued to scrutinize Casey. Harlan whistled, and they all fell in line again. Casey watched the pups follow Justice up and over barriers, over and under fences, through huge culvert-looking pipes, and lastly to the attack dummy. On command, Justice threw her formidable weight high into the chest of the first dummy. It toppled to the ground, and the pups joined in trying to shred the dummy. Harlan praised them. He put the dummy upright and commanded each of the pups to attack it. Tessa and her light-colored siblings went for the legs of the dummy, and Harlan praised each effort. It was the black pup's turn. Casey was expecting him to attack the legs like the rest had, but he leaped into the air and toppled the dummy! He was working on shredding the faux assailant's throat when Harlan called him off and praised him profusely.

He left Harlan and came to sit in front of Casey, as if to say, "How did I do?"

Casey sat down on the ground. "Wow! What a brave boy." He approached her and laid his head in her lap while she fussed over him and scratched behind his ears. She looked up at Harlan. "What's his name?"

"Tracy named him Sombra del Lobo."

"What does that mean?"

"It's Tracy's Spanish translation of Wolf's Shadow."

Casey thought the Shadow part was okay, but she wasn't sure that she liked the wolf reference. "I would like to buy him, if he is for sale."

"He definitely likes you. What does JD think about your getting a puppy?"

"JD doesn't make my decisions for me. Will you sell me Shadow or not?" She gave Harlan a wry smile and shrugged her shoulders at the terse outburst that his offhand comment had brought forth.

Casey agreed to leave Shadow for thirty days so he could learn some house manners that included house breaking. She had to agree with Tracy's assessment: it would be easier on the pup if they acclimated him to life indoors because he was used to their training methods. Casey parted with a substantial wad of cash for her new canine companion and signed up for additional training classes that included her handling the pup. She felt that he was extremely intelligent and had inherited his mother's instincts.

She had also accomplished her secondary goal of finding out more about Pete Dugan, and Tracy made arrangements for a visit with him the following day. She wasn't looking forward to a knockdown, drag-out brawl with JD about her plans. Maybe it would be more prudent not to tell him about the meeting, she thought. "Ben, let's stop for dinner in Brush before we head back to the ranch."

"Are you and JD at war again?"

Casey merely stared at him when she parked the Yukon near the front entrance of the local Mexican restaurant that Ben had suggested. She and JD had been locked in a battle of wills since he'd unexpectedly dropped in at her grandmother's during 2006. Most of it was her unwillingness to trust him. Whenever she ignored the warnings of the shades that haunted her dreams and reached out to him he rejected her, like her father before him. She couldn't articulate the depth of her emotional scars to Ben or anyone else. "I don't want to discuss JD. Let's just have dinner."

******

JD was trying to control the urge to hunt down Casey and thump Ben. He wondered what was taking them so long to get home. Harlan told him they had left his place several hours earlier. His mind was conjuring up one disaster after another until Ben checked in. JD's heard his evil sibling was on an early morning flight back to the States.

Chapter 20

To say that JD was opposed to Casey's articulated plans for the day would be as huge an understatement as that of the experts who'd claimed the Iraq debacle would last only a few months. She knew better than to share her and Tracy's real plans with him.

Casey had argued that she was entitled to a day out with a friend now and then. "We are going on a shopping spree. Tracy can give me a hand picking out some training aids and toys for Shadow. Then we may take in a movie after lunch." Packing the Yukon was the tricky part. Her bogus plans for the day should give them a head start before JD thought to check with Harlan when they failed to return.

Twenty hours later, they pulled up to the gate of a retirement community on the outskirts of Fort Wayne. Security was impressive for the gated neighborhood and an obvious perk. Fortunately, Tracy had a pass.

Her introduction to Pete Dugan was a bit disorienting. She had seen only black-and-white news photos of him taken in 1985 when she was doing online research about him and the accident. His dark hair was now silver, and there was a bit less of it. His eyes sparkled with joy at the site of his child. He peered at the world through unlined bifocals, but his eyes were still as vivid a blue as his daughter's like-colored orbs. Pete enveloped Tracy in a bear hug that sent pangs straight to Casey's heart. She could not recall a single hug or modicum of affection from her own father. JD had said that her dad doted on her, but she could not call up a single warm moment. She wondered if the trauma associated with the fatal crash had blocked her early memories, or if it was it more a matter that she had been too young at the time for those recollections to carry through to the present.

Much of the afternoon was spent huddled around the oak pedestal table in the kitchen. Pete's second wife, Charlene, served them breakfast and then lunch. The kitchen was small but functional and homey. The white cabinets were warmed with granite countertops that were a close match to the oak table and chairs. Stainless appliances were offset by a hardwood floor. Herb pots and plants decorated the window spaces.

Casey learned that Pete had met Charlene during the hearing that resulted in his DUI conviction. She's had been a young journalist at the time and had come to the conclusion Pete Dugan was being railroaded. Her story got squelched. Like her husband-to-be, she was fired from her job. After years of being blackballed and unable to gain meaningful employment, they moved to Indiana. Charlene had family in the area.

"My parents took us in, and we stayed with them for nearly a year. We purchased a small house and raised two sons. Tracy came to visit us once she went off to college."

"Charlene and I kept our heads down and concentrated on the day-to day routine of work and our kids. The deliberate destruction of your family haunted me, Casey. And when Tracy married Harlan, we met his Aunt Rosa, who added fuel to my quest for justice. So I have documented, with Charlene's assistance, the events of that fateful day. I was able to track down the driver of the truck,

Carl Strom. Carl admitted to being paid to put the fear of God into the Hoffman family. I have the tape of that conversation where he names Big Joe Gannon's foreman as the man who hired him and supplied the truck. It was common knowledge that Gannon had a crew of criminal types at his disposal to do his dirty work. He would always be somewhere with high visibility and plenty of reputable witnesses."

"That hasn't changed. He was out of the country when the attempt was made to blow JD and me into oblivion."

Casey laid out her plan, and Charlene gave her a list of high profile, online journalists who thrived on exposés.

Tracy stayed to visit for a couple of days while Casey made the trip to Ohio to visit with Andi and her little one. It could be her last chance to see her friends. She was determined to put an end to Big Joe Gannon, but more likely that he would put an end to her. She stayed overnight in Westlake and called Andi from there. Then she uploaded her mom's diary to the four online journalists who had responded to the queries that she had sent out that morning.

The sun was already high in the sky by the time Casey got her act together. Fortunately, it was less than an hour's drive to Andi and Rick's place. It was a Saturday, and Casey knew that Rick would be home. She was bracing for his tirade about traveling alone when Andi came barreling through the door, squealing and practically squeezing the life out of her.

"It's about time you came to visit us. You're late!"

Casey returned the hug. "Sorry. I overslept. I've been a bit sleep deprived lately. Where is baby Colin?"

"He's down for a nap." Andi cast a worried glance over her shoulder toward the house, then whispered. "JD arrived this morning, and he's really pissed."

"Great, I suppose that means Rick is, too."
"You got that right."
"I'm sorry, Andi, I only wanted to see you and your son before the shit hits the fan."
Andi linked arms with Casey and they walked into the lion's den.

******

JD knew he should have gone with Cassie and Tracy, but she did have a point about deserving a day out with a friend, now and then. He and Ben occupied themselves with chores, including filling in the pit carved out by the explosives. They shared lunch and then dinner. It was nearing midnight when it occurred to him that she'd lied to him. JD placed a call to Harlan, who sounded like the phone had disrupted his sleep. Tracy's husband was not in the least concerned that his wife was still absent. "She said that she was going to spend a few days with her dad. I'll give them a call in the morning to ask if Casey is with her."

JD disconnected the cell phone and stuffed the disposable device into his back pocket. He didn't see much point in getting Harlan worked up too, so he skipped the part about Tracy's car being parked in front of Casey's little house. It was a good thing he couldn't get his hands on her at the moment. Maybe he should have told her about Pete Dugan, but he didn't want to put her through what he had learned about the accident. She was stressed out enough from reading her mom's journal. JD, like Rosa, had come to the conclusion that the death of Cassie's mom and brothers had not been an accident. Bill had blamed himself for losing control of the car, and hence the death of his family. Cassie and her grandparents had always been under the impression that her parents' death was an accident. They had all thought the same prior to Tracy marrying into the Ramirez family and they met Pete at his daughter's wedding.

JD was terrified Casey would go off the deep end and decide to up her attack on Big Joe. Life sure wouldn't be worth a damn if he lost her. He was determined that loss wouldn't come to pass.

Harlan called around ten the next morning, but informed him that Cassie had already left for Ohio to visit with a friend. JD cussed a blue streak as he headed into the house to pack. Hector drove him to the airport, and then returned to the Hoffman Ranch to join his son, Ben, and a dozen more of the hands from JD's outfit to patrol the grounds and protect the Hoffman ranch while he was gone.

Rick picked him up at the Cleveland Airport. JD had barely seated himself at the table with a hot cup of coffee when Andi went flying out the front door.

Rick took one look at his friend's expression and asked, "When are you going to stop fighting it and ask her to marry you, JD?"

"I tried that a few days ago."

Rick waited for the rest, but it was obvious JD had dropped the subject. "What did she say?"

JD tried to remember the exact discussion. "She didn't let me finish and changed the subject."

"Did you or did you not ask her to marry you?" Rick watched him shake his head and shrug. He was about to ask for clarification of this proposal when Andi entered the kitchen with her arm around Casey.

JD drank in the sight of her. He experienced such relief she was well and unharmed that he forgot about his anger. "You're late!"

"So I've been told. What are you doing here?"

JD made a command decision. "I'm here for a wedding."

That was news to her. She didn't know any of her friends planning a wedding. Maybe it was someone who Andi and Rick knew that she didn't. "Who's getting married?"

JD rose from his seat opposite Rick and approached her. "We are," he informed her as he gazed into her skeptical green eyes.

"That's not funny, JD, and it's not going to happen. You turned your back on that opportunity in Virginia."

"It was the worst mistake I've made in my life, and I really was trying to protect you."

"Yeah, right!" She turned away and headed for the front door, but he followed her out to the drive. He spun her around and clasped her close to his much larger body.

"I love you, Cassie, and I want to spend the rest of my days with you."

She tried to wiggle free of his embrace. "I've heard that crap before. 'I love you' only means 'I want control over what you do and where you go.'"

"You never heard that from me."

"No. You just started ordering me around without the fancy words. Ask me again if we survive the next two weeks."

"Look, Cassie, I've loved you my whole life, and I don't want to live another day without you as mine. This is your home and all your friends are here. There will never be a better time or place."

"It takes three days from the time a person files for a license before they can get married, and today is Saturday."

He grinned. "I'm not in a hurry to get back to Colorado. Are you?"

Casey was able to delay her decision for twenty-four hours and sought the privacy of a hotel near the airport. Her temporary digs gave her access to a great in-house restaurant and room amenities including a refrigerated bar and Wi-Fi. A warm shower beckoned. Refreshed, the next step was to placate the rumbling coming from her midsection by dialing room service for a chef's salad and a cup of minestrone soup. Fortunately, a blow dryer was another perk provided by the five-star hotel. Her auburn locks were relatively dry by the time her lunch was delivered. Next on her agenda was to check the online news links that Charlene had given her. Only one of the four sites was up already, and she figured that news outlet wanted to scoop the rest. Too late to back out now, she thought. The final showdown was underway. She placed her lunch tray outside the door, and then stretched out across the double bed and zonked out.

He was standing on the same hill. Backlit by the sun, but this time she refused to reach out to him. What was the point? He always turned away from her. Instead, he began to move toward her. Her nigh shade began to take on an animal-like appearance. She blinked him into focus. The shade resembled her father! Suddenly, a large, ominous shadow covered him, and when the shadow lifted from atop his form, her dad's image was replaced with the likeness of a young Pete Dugan, who continued toward her. The shadow solidified a bit and took on a bear-like form that appeared to swipe at the man descending the hill. The bear shadow fell back, as if it had been struck a painful blow, and the man moved closer. Her shadow man had taken on the likeness of JD. The huge bear shadow backed away from him, but turned to swoop down on her. JD's form faded and reappeared as a huge black wolf that sprung up to send the bear to the ground at her feet. She heard a shrill scream!

Casey bolted into a sitting position, still screaming. Her heartbeat slowed and the quaking of her drenched body subsided when she realized the shrill sound echoing through the room was only the house phone and not someone's last death throws. She wondered why on earth such a thought would suddenly pop into her mind. She snatched up the receiver to silence the annoying sound. JD was on the other end of the line. "Hi Cassie, I made reservations for dinner at seven downstairs. I'll pick you up in thirty minutes."

"JD. JD! Damn." He'd hung up before she could refuse or even ask where he was. The infuriating man was dogging her trail.

A half hour passed in a blur while she showered to remove the odor of sweat and fear that clung to her following her nightmare. Toweling off, she wondered why the bad dreams were haunting her once more. They'd not plagued her since her return to her family's ranch. Something was different about this dream, but exactly what was lost when she was catapulted back to reality. Casey had barely slipped into her burgundy slacks and settled the pale pink and burgundy print tunic over her head when he rapped on the door. He looked more rested than he had that morning. As usual he was decked out in jeans and a blue plaid shirt, but the rough-out boots were new, and she didn't remember ever seeing the suede suit coat before. She let the door hang open for him to enter while she turned away to step into a pair of wine-colored leather pumps and snatch up the matching clutch. Casey opted to let her hair hang free due to lack of time to fool with it. Once again, the thought crossed her mind to get it cut.

She returned to where he stood positioned in the partially open door with his eyes roving over her. "Okay, JD, what are you doing here?" She couldn't help the exasperated quality of her voice.

"We both need to eat. This seemed a more appropriate place to discuss our situation than at Rick and Andi's place." He didn't utter another word as they entered the elevator, or as the hostess escorted them to the dining room.

She took note of his deepening frown lines and the determined set of his jaw. She held off until the waiter left with their order. "You promised to give me until tomorrow evening to have this discussion."

"No. I promised to wait for your answer to my marriage proposal until tomorrow. I want to discuss what you found out when you met with Tracy's father."

"You knew all along about Pete, and you never said a word about him to me." Flashing green eyes clashed with blue ones that were quickly becoming glacial.

JD bided his time while the salad and rolls were served, and the server vacated. "I didn't think you could handle it. Also, I was worried you would go off half-cocked and get yourself killed."

She didn't answer him. Instead, she tackled her salad and refused to look at him again or acknowledge his assessment of her response to the knowledge gleaned from Pete Dugan that her family's death was not an accident, but a planned execution.

He knew in his gut she had already come up with a plan of attack when she didn't take exception to his accusation. "Okay, Cassie, out with it. What are you planning to do with the information from Pete?"

"I don't plan on doing anything with it. It's not my story to tell." She still didn't look at him. He was too darn perceptive, and she sure wasn't going to provoke him. "Can't we have a pleasant meal without you giving me the third degree? I knew you wouldn't be happy with my plans to visit with Pete. You would have try to stop me, so I didn't tell you."

JD bit back the urge to call her a bald-faced liar, and acquiesced to her request for an enjoyable meal. He was exhausted and struggling to keep his temper under wraps. She was probably just as beat, judging from the dark circles beneath her eyes. He figured waiting until morning wouldn't make much difference at this point.

The rest of the meal passed peacefully, but the tension sapped any enjoyment of the excellent cuisine.

Casey made it back to her room, which turned out to be only four down the hall from where JD had parked his frame nearly five hours earlier. She kicked off her shoes, latched onto a mini bottle of wine, snagged a glass, and settled down to troll the Internet. All four news outlets had posted her mom's diary, and they all carried Charlene Dugan's old interview with Pete. Both articles went viral. Big Joe's skeletons rattled around the globe. Casey's satisfaction was short-lived as she contemplated JD's reaction to the cyber attack that she and Charlene had initiated.

One more little bottle of wine, and she slid under the bedclothes a couple of hours before dawn. Her eyes had barely closed when the phone blasted in her ear. She blinked and struggled to focus. Bright light rays were filtering through the partially drawn drapes when she snatched the receiver off its cradle. "What?" she growled at the party on the other end. Her voice was raw and several octaves lower; the sound was foreign to her own ears. She hung up when she heard JD's voice. Then Casey once more removed the handset, laid it on the table, and pulled the sheets up over her head. She wasn't ready to deal with him yet. Maybe if she could get a little more sleep, she would be able to face the inevitable fallout.

******

JD opted to give her some space after he coerced the day manager of the hotel to open the door to Casey's room. She was burrowed under the covers, but still breathing. He wasn't about to wake her and start a row this morning; it would only give her more reason to refuse his proposal.

Several hours later, he had contacted Tracy to set up a flight out to Denver for her. "Tracy, give Harlan a call to pick you up at the airport. Cassie and I will also be flying back in a couple of days."

Rick had arranged to have the Yukon crushed at a local scrap yard. "Does Casey know about your plan to make her SUV disappear, JD?"

"No. I think she was avoiding me this morning, and I let her."

"Did you get a look at what is on the Internet? Christ! Andi couldn't stop crying, and finally showed me what had upset her. Casey has declared all-out war on Big Joe."

"Yeah, I think the message sent via Bob Jackson that Big Joe considered the rape charges frivolous stoked her ire. She evidently became even more enraged after visiting with Pete Dugan, and decided to attack him on the social media front instead of counting on the legal system."

"What's the next step?"

"Cassie and I need to get married, and we all need to assemble a united front. Establish a good alibi for the next couple of weeks, Rick." His friend nodded his understanding.

Casey had already arrived at the O'Bannon household before JD and Rick returned from their battle strategy meeting. She was cuddling baby Colin and bouncing him on her knee while his mom put together a chicken salad for their lunch.

Andi had regained her composure and calmed down several notches by the time her friend arrived, but Casey's anxiety level spiked exponentially. It appeared the reason for Rick's absence from home on a Sunday was that he and JD were holed up somewhere discussing strategy. As a result of her and Charlene's plastering his nefarious deeds all over the Internet, they expected a counterattack by Big Joe. Casey knew it was a matter of hours, a day at most, before JD found out what she had done. She figured Bob Jackson would have an apoplexy and spill the beans; she hadn't considered that her best friend would sound the alarm first.

Andi placed the salad plates on the table, took the baby from Casey's arms, and went to put him down for an afternoon nap. She returned within a few minutes to attack her salad and her friend. "Okay, Casey, what have you decided?"

Casey pondered the subject of the open-ended question while she chewed the grape and almond loaded salad, then washed it down with a swig from her glass of water. "Are you referring to my legal case against Big Joe?"

"You know I'm talking about JD's proposal, right here in this kitchen, yesterday!" Her aggravated tone was punctuated with a clank of her fork as she tossed it onto the glass plate while she glared at Casey.

"I'm weighing the pros and cons." Casey shrugged her shoulders and refocused on her lunch.

"God, Casey. Haven't you ever made a mistake with the best of intentions? Give the guy a break. He's expecting an answer today."

"Thanks for lunch, Andi. I think it's time for me to leave." Casey rose from the table gave her friend a hug, retrieved her bag and laptop, and headed out the side door to the Yukon parked in the drive.

Andi followed her out. "What am I supposed to tell JD when he returns?"

Casey slid behind the wheel and powered down the window. "You don't have to tell him anything. He knows where I am. He tracked me down yesterday."

The truth was, she still couldn't get past the crushed hopes caused by the major male players in her life. Mark had become overbearing. He'd tried to dominate her life and control her once she became engaged to him, and when he couldn't, he had hit her in a drunken rage on their last night together. Her father had abandoned her, and JD had done the same when she ignored the internal warning bells and gave him her heart. She wondered if she could spend the rest of her life with the post-Iraq JD without it ending in violence. He had a propensity to be overprotective and an equal tendency to bark orders at her. That character trait was understandable with all the years of his life spent in the military. However, she wasn't one of his recruits or a hired ranch hand; she tended get her back up and defy his dictates.

She sighed, resting her throbbing forehead on the steering wheel while she waited for one of the valets to park her vehicle.

As she entered the elevator, the thought flitted through her mind that both of their days were running short. The world as they knew it was about to end with all the impact of the IED that had forever altered JD. Perhaps they both needed something or someone to believe in, even if it was the unlikely chance at a future together.

Chapter 21

May sixth of 2010, Casey and JD were wed at the little church she had attended with her grandmother. Andi and Rick stood up with them and had secured the church hall for the wedding reception. Gram's friend Millie sat on the bride's side in the family pew. The rest of that row of seats was filled with Susan, George, his two sisters, and their husbands. Casey was speechless. She didn't know whether to hug Andi or kick her in the butt. She even posted a notice in the local newspaper. So much for staying under the radar, Casey thought.

All of her old friends were in attendance when she and JD exchanged matching gold bands. The beams of the vaulted ceiling vibrated and the stain glass windows rattled from the exuberant applause and whoops of the assemblage as JD kissed his new wife. One of the folks occupying the groom side of the church turned out to be a photographer, so in addition to the smartphone photos that were, no doubt, already circulating on friends' Facebook pages, a set of professional photos would document the occasion.

JD appeared to be a normal, happy groom, and he was a dashing figure in his rented charcoal gray tux with satin lapels. His ivory vest and tie matched the ivory gown that Cassie had chosen at the shop down the street from where her old studio had been. The ball gown was a sleeveless creation with a high, banded waist beneath her breasts; then it flowed to the floor in a smooth, modified A-line. A like-colored lace bolero jacket and ivory pumps completed the elegant look. Her hair was swept up into a sophisticated style that she would never be able to duplicate. Her stepmother had accomplished the amazing feat with her auburn tresses. Casey tried to relax and enjoy the day, but she was sure that Big Joe would get word of their nuptials before the day was out. The next event that their friends and family would be planning for them would be their funeral.

She shook off the morbid thought as they made their way down the aisle toward the front entrance. Casey wondered again about the stern, tough-looking men who occupied the pews on the opposite side of the church from her friends sat. They took up two rows behind Rick and Andi's more normal appearing friends. Where they the security people that Rick worked with, or were they ex-military friends of her new husband?

Casey recognized the set jaws and steely-eyed look of those men; the facial expressions where similar to the look that Rick had leveled at their nemesis in court. JD had that look while watching Trooper and Justice play with the unsuccessful bomber. She greeted each cordially as she was introduced. It turned out that they were a mix of former marines and private security types.

JD's little wife had a good buzz on from all the free-flowing champagne that her Oregon family had contributed to the reception. Not hampered by the bubbly she'd ingested, JD made quick work of removing his tux. Meanwhile, she couldn't seem to manage the small zipper at the back of her gown. He came to the rescue and had her out of it in a flash. The room began to spin, and the last coherent thought that crossed Casey's mind was that she had way too much to drink. Then again, it could have been the passionate, tongue-thrusting lip lock from her new husband that tilted her world.

She was sure her uninhibited sexual foreplay and earth-shattering orgasms of their wedding night was a side effect of her champagne binge. That theory was debunked over the short two-day honeymoon they spent making instant replays. Room service got a lot of use, and only occasionally did they venture downstairs to dine or use the pool. Sunday night, they made love like the world would end the following day. They had invited Andi and her taciturn husband out to celebrate her friend's very first Mother's Day earlier that evening.

Casey slept from the time the plane lifted off the tarmac at Hopkins until it touched down in Denver. Rick's uncharacteristic silence the prior evening radiated his level of stress and had ground its way into her very bones. JD had made it his mission to relieve her anxiety with mind-blowing sex that began when he joined her for her evening shower.

Casey would have fallen on the shower floor when he applied his soapy fingers to her already tender breasts and her knees buckled. Thankfully, her tormenter had a good hold on her. He stimulated every erogenous place on her body and then JD lifted her up—much the same as he had done that rainy night on Gram's front lawn—to consummate their rain dance started four years earlier He spent the rest of the night in their marriage bed driving her past the tenuous hold she had on reality.

The true consequences of the latest battlefront she'd opened in their ongoing war with Big Joe was about to erupt in Northeastern Colorado with all the impact of a major earthquake.

Chapter 22

Harrison bolted for the bathroom so quickly that he upended the chair in front of his desk. Whenever he thought it was safe to lift his head from the facedown encounter with the porcelain throne, cramps and prompted him to return. Dry heaves plagued him for a time, and he wept like a small child.

His sounds of distress drew his brother to his side. "Are you sick or hung over?"

He couldn't articulate the scope of his anguish, so he didn't answer. He splashed some cold water on his face after rinsing the foul taste from his mouth. "Come with me, Spence," he finally said in a shaky, raw voice as he carelessly dropped a damp hand-towel onto the bathroom floor. He returned to his desk in the room that served as their office. It now had a very masculine décor, and no longer resembled the nursery it had once been. He woke up his laptop, which had gone to sleep during his prolonged absence. "A friend sent me an e-mail with a link that has a couple of mind-blowing articles about our father. Have you seen this?"

Spencer retrieved his chair from the duplicate walnut desk where he had been working on some of his and Harrison's investment portfolios. He settled next to his brother and began to read the diary of Kathryn Hoffman. He took a break following that gut-wrenching read to splash bourbon into a couple of crystal tumblers. He drained one and refilled it before returning to his seat to tackle the article submitted by a Charlene Dugan. He handed one glass to his younger brother. Side by side, they digested the bourbon and Pete Dugan's recollection of the accident. The article documented the failure of the law to follow up on leads on the white truck involved, and the persecution of both Pete and Charlene.

"Christ, Harry, no wonder you got sick." Spencer had a vague recollection of the adults in the memoirs posted online, but he vividly remembered Billy and Carson. They had played together as young children. He and Carson had spent more time together; less than a year separated their ages, while Billy had spent most of his time with JD. "Harry, do you remember the Hoffman kids? You would have been only about eight when they died."

"You mean when they were murdered?"

"Be careful who you say that to. The accusations are only a couple of online stories at this point."

"I don't remember the Hoffman kids, but I remember that Grandpa Jim had no use for our father. I also remember Dad's hatred of Uncle JD, and how it escalated over the years. I remember him dragging us back here from Grandpa Victor's farm."

"I never told you this, Harry, but I overheard him threaten Mom's parents and their farm, if she fought him over custody of us."

"How could you stomach his lies that Mom had run off with another man and didn't want us tagging along when you knew the truth?"

"It was hard at times, but I was worried he would go after our mom and our grandparents if I said anything. The hardest part was faking the loyal son while I prayed that each breath he took would be his last, and we would finally be free of him."

"Where is he now, Spence? I haven't seen him since he returned home."

"He had me drop him at Pratt's office in Denver. I guess they're working on strategies of how to deal with Casey Hoffman. She filed rape charges against him and is trying to revoke the lease the old man holds on her ranch."

"Do you think he knows about the online attack, Spence?"

"It's probably only a matter of time until someone works up the nerve to tell him. Could be he already knows, but he can't blame us for not informing him when he isn't home and won't accept phone calls from us when he's in conference."

******

"What the hell do you mean they're on vacation?" Big Joe slammed his fist on Pratt's desk and fought the urge to break his lawyer's nose.

Roland Pratt had inherited the Joe Gannon account from his retired father. Roland was sure the elder Pratt gave up his practice so he wouldn't have to deal with Big Joe any longer. "We were informed of their absence when my paralegal tried to set up an appointment for us. Bob Jackson informed me when I made a personal call that 'since Big Joe considers this a trivial matter, my clients decided to take a short vacation.' Jackson seemed to think that they would be returning in a couple of days."

"Find out when and get this done, or I'll find a more aggressive law firm."

"Yes, sir," Roland answered, but he was silently hoping that Big Joe would take his business elsewhere.

Big Joe went from his meeting with Pratt directly to the Sheriff's office to touch bases with Tucker. Every speed limit along the way was shredded.

Sheriff Tucker scalded his throat with a nervous gulp of freshly brewed coffee. That absent-minded burning of his esophagus was a direct result of the hostility radiating from Big Joe Gannon as he barged through the main door. All conversations ceased. Deputies, dispatchers, and clerks held their breath. Gannon made his entrance during shift change, and once he cleared the entrance, those lucky enough to be off duty made a hasty exit.

It was obvious to Billy Tucker and every person in the room, that the man was in the throes of a monumental rage. In an effort to break the stilted silence, the sheriff moved forward. "Afternoon, Big Joe, to what do we owe this pleasure?"

"Cut the small talk, Tucker. This is business." Gannon barged past him and stormed down the hall to the sheriff's private office.

The sheriff set his mug of coffee down, and turned toward the room at large. "Your shift has begun. Get to work." Then he followed Big Joe. The SOB had commandeered his chair and had his snakeskin boots propped on his desk.

"It's about time you got your sorry ass down here," Big Joe growled as the sheriff parked his portly frame in one of the two chairs in front of the desk.

"What can I do for you, Big Joe?"

"You can get your fat ass out to the Hoffman ranch and place some new bugs! That's what you can do for me. I want to know what they are up to."

"Mr. Gannon, with all due respect, I wouldn't be able to get near that place without being shot."

Big Joe sprung to his feet, sending the rolling leather desk chair sailing into the wall hard enough to rattle the windows. He leaned across the desk to tower over the seated sheriff. "That's a load of crap, Tucker. I have it on good authority that JD and Casey are on vacation and aren't expected back for another day or two."

"That may well be true, but I already tried to do what you so politely requested when I got word that JD took a flight out of

Denver. It appeared he was in pursuit of Casey, who'd taken off to parts unknown. They may not be there, but that ranch is an armed camp complete with twenty-four-seven patrols. I guess JD isn't taking any chances since he thwarted the bomb attack."

"You're not much good to me anymore, Tucker. Looks like I need to find a new candidate for sheriff next election, one that has some nerve." With that declaration, Big Joe left in a more agitated state than when he'd arrived.

Billy Tucker watched him depart and hoped the red face and bulging eyes were signs of a stroke. He had been wrestling with telling Big Joe about the damaging information circulating on the Internet, but he no longer felt a responsibility to enlighten him. It was time to do this job and let the voters decide his fate. Big Joe had just burned this bastion of support to the ground.

****

Big Joe added another set of rubber tread marks to the circular drive as his new silver Beemer screeched to a halt. He flung the door open and stormed into the house bellowing for his son. "Spencer!"

Spence assessed his father's mood as he walked into the elder's office. As usual he was into another decanter of bourbon. "What has you in such a jolly mood?"

"Don't give me any of your sarcastic lip. You're too much like your mother at times."

Spence shrugged his shoulders and grinned. His mom claimed that he not only looked like his dad had as a young man, but also possessed Big Joe's vindictive nature. "So what do you want?"

"I have some matters to discuss with you and your brother. Go find him."

"Sorry, but Harry isn't here."

"Where the hell is he?"

"Grandpa Victor is in the hospital, and Harrison went to help Grandma out with the farm while he's recuperating. We tried to phone you before he left, but you were in conference with Pratt and wouldn't take our call."

Spencer ducked as his father hurled the crystal decanter in his direction. Glass and bourbon exploded on the wainscoted wall behind him. "That boy is useless around this place. It's a sad state of affairs when I can't depend on my own sons."

Spencer's temper was nudging at his stoic façade. "Harry knows you find him lacking. Do you really blame him for going where he is valued and can contribute?" Harrison possessed the sandy hair, tall, slim build, engaging smile, and hazel eyes of his maternal grandfather. "I'm here. What's so urgent?"

"Have you heard anything about Casey Hoffman revoking the remainder of lease that her father gave me?" Big Joe scrutinized his eldest son, and wondered if he was as loyal as he appeared.

"I've heard rumors. Casey hasn't been silent in regard to her hatred of you, and it seems to have escalated since someone attempted to blow her and JD up. Of course, you wouldn't know anything about that."

Big Joe refused to rise to the bait that his son tossed at him. "I want you to go over to the Hoffman ranch when that pair of troublemakers return from their vacation trip. See if you can get them to give you an extension or a new lease on the property. Casey may be willing to negotiate with you. It is common knowledge that she doesn't want the ranch, but refuses to let me buy it."

"Yeah…well, it's also common knowledge that JD owns half of that ranch, and he'll never sell out to you." JD hated Big Joe almost as much as Spencer hated his alcoholic, bullying father.

"This place will be yours one day. Take some initiative! Work out a deal with Casey to buy or lease the place. I'll take care of getting JD out of the picture."

"Why JD and not Casey?"

"JD is the cog in the wheel. Without his influence, she would have sold the ranch back when Bill cashed it in."

Spencer couldn't help the snort that escaped, and he noted his father's deepening scowl. Big Joe had always underestimated women. It was obvious that his Dad hadn't seen or caught wind of the Internet buzz. "I'll take a run over there when they return."

Big Joe was out like a light when Spencer arrived at the long-term parking lot at the Denver airport and caught a flight out to confer with his mother and brother.

Chapter 23

Hector and Rosa were waiting at the baggage collection when Casey and JD landed in Denver. The newlyweds arrived a mere two days after Spencer boarded a flight to Virginia on a round-trip ticket. A rapid-fire Spanish conversation started the minute they left the terminal and continued on the ride home.

It was evident to Casey that either the others were trying to hide events from her, or they reverted to speaking that language when stressed out. It appeared that Big Joe was making veiled threats against the couple and their son as well as against Harlan and Tracy. Casey continued to stare out the window at the traffic while she eavesdropped on their discussion. Her Spanish was a bit rusty, but she understood most of the exchange.

JD's Spanish was a little slower than Rosa's and easier to follow. Casey attempted to translate his question. "Do you think Big Joe has seen what is circulating on the online news sites?"

"Our son doesn't believe that he has." Hector went on to explain that Ben thought that if Big Joe had gotten wind of the articles, he would have struck out by now. Casey thought it curious that not a soul in Big Joe's circle, including his sons, had bothered to inform him of the articles that had gone viral. However, it was only a matter of time until the TV or newspaper journalists latched on to the exposés and decided to run with the story.

They weren't unpacked yet when Bob Jackson phoned. JD ended the conversation and then turned toward his curious wife. "Ten tomorrow morning in Bob's office. Big Joe will be there to discuss your grievances."

"Grievances? Is he kidding, JD?"

"I think it would be wise to go to Denver tonight."

Casey ate very lightly the following morning. A hot cup of tea and an English muffin was about all her jumpy stomach could manage, but JD chose the biggest breakfast on the menu. It was obvious to her that her new husband was stalling, and she wondered if his deliberate attempt to arrive late for their confrontation with Big Joe had anything to do with his late night phone call. He checked an incoming text message and finally asked for the bill. Their scheduled appointment had passed by forty-five minutes when he paid the check and tossed the tip on the table.

*****

Big Joe paced the waiting area at Jackson, Vosar and Day's law offices. He scowled at Roland Pratt, who was hiding behind a Time magazine and ignoring him. Big Joe planned to fire Pratt's butt following this farce of a meeting. He'd arrived early to forestall any attempt at a last-minute strategy conference between Bob Jackson and his clients. He'd expected to be ushered into Bob's office. Instead, he sat cooling his heels as if he was a person of little consequence. Only the realization that the slight was an attempt to provoke him allowed him to rein in his temper.

At eleven-thirty Mary led him and his lawyer back to Bob's sanctum, where they were greeted with the sight of JD and Casey relaxing, sipping coffee, and chatting with Spencer. The three hadn't come past him. He tried to subdue his ire, pasted on a relaxed demeanor, and then attempted to smile at his son. Spence had vanished a couple of days previously. His father wondered where he had gone and why he was in Bob's office. Icy fingers played up his spine, his heart raced, and he felt the blood beating at his temples. "I wasn't expecting you to be in on this meeting, Spence." He tried to sound his normal, brusque self as he seated himself next to his son.

"Where else would I be today? As you so recently reminded me, I am to step into your shoes one day, and therefore I should show some initiative in the operation of our business ventures."

Bob broke the stare down between the father and son by introducing JD and Casey to Roland Pratt. Roland decided to get to the point before his unpredictable client exploded in a fit of rage and made matters worse. "Mr. Jackson, my client is a busy man, as am I. We have been kept waiting for nearly two hours and would like to get down to the airing of your client's grievances."

Casey let out an unladylike snort at the word "grievance". JD took her hand and gave her a look that warned her to keep quiet. Bob set the tone for the rest of the legal maneuverings. "My client is here to address the assault on her mother by Mr. Joseph Gannon."

Big Joe jumped from his chair and rounded on Casey. "This is insane! You don't have an ounce of proof that will hold up in court."

JD stood toe-to-toe with his elder sibling, effectively blocking any further advance toward Casey.

Bob took Big Joe's attorney to task. "Mr. Pratt, please control your client." Once everyone was seated, he continued. "As a matter of fact, we do have evidence that will hold up in court and substantiate the accounts set down in Kathryn Hoffman's journal. Big Joe has supplied us with a DNA lab report claiming Cassandra Hoffman as his biological daughter. Without this DNA report, we would not be able to proceed with a rape case this old. Now, should your client wish to admit that the lab report on file is bogus, we may be open to dropping the rape charges."

"I would like to confer with my client. We will be in touch."

"Mr. Pratt, your client has twenty-four hours to come to a decision. At that time we will file the DNA report and Kathryn's journal with the DA's office when we file a charge of rape against Mr. Joseph Gannon."

Big Joe sent the plush armchair flying when he rounded on Casey and JD. "This isn't over!" he bellowed like a wounded bear.

JD leveled his cold, laser-like gaze on Big Joe. "Yeah, it is. One way or another, we're finished living under your ominous shadow."

Big Joe stopped at the door that Pratt had moments before exited, expecting his client to follow him. Instead, he stood confronting JD. "Are you threatening me?" JD didn't say another word, but kept staring at him with those disturbing, ice-blue eyes. Big Joe felt Spencer take hold of his arm and guide him out the door. His thoughts were busy running through his list of minions. Who among them could take on JD?

Spencer confronted his father in the elevator. "Dad, you need to get a grip on your temper and your excessive drinking. I would advise you to admit that there could be an error made at the lab on Casey's DNA report. Perhaps JD will overlook the fact that you falsified a similar report on him after Grandpa Jim passed away."

"What makes you think JD will let that information slide?"

"It would be in his best interest. In case you didn't notice, they were wearing matching wedding bands."

Pratt put in his little barb as the doors swung open in the lobby: "Spencer is correct; I also noticed the wedding bands. This vendetta with your brother is blinding you to greater dangers."

"What greater danger? Quit beating around the bush, Pratt, and spit it out!"

"It has been brought to my attention that along with the rape charge, there is the potential for murder charges to be filed against you," his attorney informed him.

"Who told you such nonsense?"

Spencer answered, "I told him, and it's not nonsense. You need to see what the online news outlets are circulating. The word is that more and more complaints, along with additional witnesses, have sprung up to document your nefarious deeds. It looks like it's time to pay the piper!"

Big Joe felt his blood boil as he read Kathryn's journal posted for the world to see. His early political aspirations that had been dashed by Melinda's defection were mentioned. His rapes of Kathryn and Val were both unearthed. He wondered if JD had knowledge of Kathryn's documentation of his early life, or if Casey Hoffman had instigated this attack. The vivid account of the crash that killed Bill Hoffman and his family elicited even more outrage. How many people knew about these reports? Spencer claimed that Harrison had left home for Virginia after reading this rubbish. Big Joe fought to control his growing paranoia. Spencer had also claimed that both he and Harry had tried to warn their father, but he would not take their calls. "They still can't prove I had anything to do with any of it."

"While it may be true you have airtight alibis for the events listed, your hired assassins have pointed fingers that lead straight to your door, Daddy."

******

"Now what do we do?" Casey was at a loss. She had expected Big Joe to capitulate and at least admit that perhaps an error had been made at the lab.

Bob Jackson recognized the deadly intent in JD's demeanor. The attorney came up with a plan. "At this juncture, it's best to wait the twenty-four hours and then proceed from there. Tonight, I would like to take you out to celebrate your new status as a married couple." To his relief, they agreed to meet him for dinner at seven. The celebratory dinner in a few hours would give JD time to cool down instead of instigating a showdown with his half-brother.

Big Joe was in his Denver office calling in favors and swilling bourbon while Casey and JD shared prime rib and a few drinks with Bob Jackson. How quickly the rats flee the sinking ship, Big Joe thought. All those he had placed in positions of power refused his calls; and the covert operatives and criminals he'd recently employed declined any new assignments from him. The noose was tightening. He downed another tumbler and then refilled it as he peered into the shadowy recesses of the room. He swore he heard a threatening growl, but all he saw were two yellow eyes reflected in darkness. He lit every light in the room to hold the shadows at bay.

He decided to cut his losses and made several efforts to dial Pratt's number from his iPhone before he succeeded. Less impaired, he may have remembered to check the contact list instead of fumbling with the keypad. "Pratt," he barked, "meet with Bob Jackson at the scheduled time. Tell them that we have discovered that a mistake was made at the lab. Also inform him the results will take a while to be checked. I will give you further instructions in the morning." He intended to be well out of the country by noon tomorrow when Pratt met with Bob Jackson. Bob had joined his two clients on Big Joe's hit list. Once he settled in abroad, it wouldn't be hard to find a mercenary or two willing to earn a large paycheck.

Chapter 24

Big Joe woke facedown across his desk in the hours before dawn. Head swimming, he struggled to right himself in his chair and slowly blinked the still lit room into focus; his bloodshot eyes zeroed in on the familiar form of his eldest son. Spence was sitting in the rust-colored wing chair opposite him, sipping a tumbler of bourbon while blatantly taking inventory of his father.

Spencer raised his glass in a mock salute. "Hair of the dog?"

Big Joe inclined his head slightly to accept the offered drink from his overly solicitous son. By nature he was suspicious, but he needed the bracing drink. He found his voice after imbibing half the bourbon handed to him. "What are you doing here, Spencer?"

"Harrison called me this morning to say that Grandpa Victor was hauled away in an ambulance. It appears he will be hospitalized for a prolonged period. Bottom line, Harry will be staying in Virginia indefinitely. I checked your room, thinking the phone may have woken you, but lo and behold, you weren't there. The office seemed the most likely place to find you. I know you have an appointment late morning, so I came to give you moral support."

Big Joe checked his watch: dawn was an hour off, and he had a lot to do. "I've left instructions for Pratt to conduct the negotiations. We agreed that my presence would only aggravate the situation, and I have important business I left unfinished when I returned to straighten out these ridiculous accusations."

Spencer had become adept at reading between the lines of his father's bull. "In other words, you're hightailing it out of U. S. jurisdiction."

"I have to drive home for my passport and a few other essentials, so by the time Pratt meets with Jackson I will be well out in international air space on a private jet. I'm leaving the ranch and business interests in Colorado to you. Pratt has the paperwork to transfer those holdings into your name."

Spencer stood and moved toward the decanter of bourbon, poured two fresh glasses and handed one to his father. "What about Harry?" he asked as he occupied his previous chair.

"Harrison has made his choice, and he'll have to live with the consequences."

His son didn't argue his brother's case; he raised his glass in salute then drained it, and Big Joe did the same. He then left the office for home with the knowledge that Spencer would stand in his place at the lawyer's meeting later that day.

As soon as his father left the office, Spencer made two calls from Big Joe's landline: one to Virginia and the other to a local mobile phone. The last thing he did before he left his father's office was to pour the remaining bourbon down the drain, rinse out the decanter, and refill it with a freshly opened bottle from the private stock. He cleaned the tumblers they'd used, locked the place up, and went to have breakfast in a restaurant where he was well known. His father was correct in his earlier observation that Spencer was a chip off the old block: he had learned to cover his tracks well.

******

Casey bolted upright, soaked with sweat. She was trembling to a degree that her teeth were chattering. Try as she might, she could not recall the nightmare that had wreaked havoc on her physical being. She looked to JD for comfort, but his side of the queen size bed was unoccupied. She put her feet onto the plush carpet of the suite they had occupied for the past two nights, flicked on the bedside light, and padded toward the bathroom where a faint light shone beneath the door. She knocked and called to him, but there was no response. A nightlight illuminated the unoccupied room; it was eerie, and a sense of foreboding replaced the concern about her elusive dream.

She found a note taped above the double sink on the mirror that spanned the length of the counter.

Cassie,

I couldn't sleep, so I went to the gym and will drop by the pool before breakfast.

JD

She read the note a couple more times before attempting to wash away the lingering chill in a warm shower. Dressed, she pulled back the thick drapes and saw the sun peeking over the mountains. The view was much the same as the first time she'd stayed at this hotel; it was the night she'd first met JD, his nefarious brother, and Bob Jackson. She couldn't shake the irony. In this room, only two floors above where she'd stayed in 2006, they were gearing up for a final showdown.

JD was not in the dining room when she arrived at eight. She ordered a hot cup of tea and a bear-claw while she waited for her tardy husband. His recent text message notified her that he had a couple of phone calls to make, but he would meet her for breakfast at eight. So where was he?

Chapter 25

Joseph Gannon's day was not off to an auspicious start. The simple task of driving home had become a major headache, which had added to his crappy mood. Someone had smacked into his Beamer during the night, and it was leaking fluids all over the parking lot. Spencer had already left the office when he returned to arrange for a tow and a loner car. The old black Lincoln was a monster left over from the 1980s; it barreled down the steep grades like a ten-ton truck and steered about as well. Big Joe found it difficult to back off his normal pedal-to-the-metal—to hell with speed limits—style of driving.

"Damn! I don't need stupid drivers in my way this morning," he grumbled while adjusting the visor to assist his sunglasses in warding off the glare of the rising sun. A white van came out of the blinding light and nearly sideswiped him. When he glanced into the rearview mirror, the road was empty. He thought the driver must have been hauling ass to disappear from sight that quickly. He struggled to clear his mind. The thought occurred to him that getting wasted last night wasn't the brightest thing he'd ever done. His innate sense of paranoia kicked in; had his son put something in his drink that could give him hallucinations? He never considered the years of alcohol abuse could be responsible. His jumbled thought process reasoned that Spencer hadn't anything to gain by drugging him. He blocked the doubts from his mind and began to fixate on how he was going to make JD and Casey suffer for making him a fugitive.

He was traveling too fast when he hit the downgrade. Big Joe applied the break to slow the descent of the Town Car. Brake drums screeched in protest, and the odor of burning steel assaulted his nostrils. He let out a relieved sigh when the great, lumbering beast slowed its headlong plunge down the steep incline. His reprieve was short lived. A white pickup equipped with a huge, black cowcatcher smacked the rear of his vehicle. He kept his foot on the brake as he glanced into the rearview mirror. He recognized the truck as one of his and tried to get a view of the driver, but the sun reflecting off the windshield made identification impossible. The truck rammed the Lincoln with more force. Once more, he growled like an enraged bear while spewing cuss words, too foul to repeat, into the crisp mountain air.

Big Joe calculated the emergency truck turn-off to be a quarter of a mile ahead on the downgrade. There, he could pull off and identify the maniac in the pickup. He misjudged the curve in the road, and the Lincoln shuddered when its right side scraped along the guardrail. Heart racing, Big Joe fought for control while keeping one eye on the assailant behind him. He hit the brake hard as he stared at the sight of five people linked hand in hand, blocking the road. At first glance, they appeared as silhouettes backlit by the sun. He blinked to ward off what he thought had to be a case of heebie-jeebies from his excessive drink. As he refocused, the shadow people took on recognizable faces. JD linked hands with Harrison, who held the hand of Pete Dugan, and Spencer was the link between Pete and Bill Hoffman that completed the chain. Kathryn and her sons stood to the rear of the human roadblock.

He knew Harrison was in Virginia, and Bill and his family had been dead a long time, so Big Joe decided that JD, Pete, and Spencer were also figments of his over-stimulated imagination. He floored the accelerator to plow through them, and as he expected, they vanished before he hit them. He was feeling unreasonably elated when he got another whack from the rear that sent him spinning into the opposite lane. He couldn't control the Lincoln as it slid into the path of a huge, black semi, which transformed into a large black wolf. The animal pounced onto the hood and snarled at him as he took his last ride over the side of the mountain.

******

Casey was surprised to see Spencer arrive in the company of Roland Pratt. Neither Bob nor JD thought his presence instead of Big Joe's was noteworthy. The attorneys were working out the details of nullifying the DNA report while Spencer signed the paperwork Bob had prepared, revoking the remainder of the lease on the Hoffman ranch.

Big Joe's remains were found two days later when some passerby noticed a break in the guardrail and reported it. Not a soul went looking for him. It was said he was on his way out of the country to somewhere that he couldn't be extradited.

Big Joe's funeral was reasonably well attended, with the conspicuous absence of family other than Spencer. As the heir apparent, he took on the duty of making the arrangements. As soon as his father was buried, he boarded a flight to Virginia.

Chapter 26

Shadow sat patiently between Casey and her brother George while they shared breakfast with JD. The pup knew it was the best position for a handout. Neither JD nor Ben, who were sharing the morning meal, was a likely prospect. Casey slipped him a yummy slice of bacon.

JD scowled at her. "You will ruin him by making a lapdog out of him."

"Give it a rest, JD. I haven't held him in my lap. He only rests his head there when I'm working on the computer or reading."

"Are the two of you going to argue all morning?" George inquired.

"Nope, little brother, as soon as JD and Ben finish stuffing their faces and hitch the trailer to one of the trucks, we'll head over to the sale."

JD stomped out the door with Ben and George on his boot heels. Casey scraped the remaining bacon into Shadow's bowl. JD had been doing a lot better since they were out from under the threat of Big Joe. He had fewer flashbacks, and he was more comfortable on the highways, but he still wouldn't drive off their combined ranches.

It was mid-August, and George would be departing for college within days. He'd bonded with JD while he spent the summer at the ranch. Casey figured it was a unique experience for George to be in the company of men for a change. Her thought process was disrupted by the sound of the truck horn. She stashed the last plate into the dishwasher, flicked it on and ran to retrieve her checkbook. She stuffed it into the rear pocket of her jeans, which were getting really snug. "Come, Shadow," she called as she snatched her ball cap from the peg near the door of her newly finished kitchen.

JD looked at her and then sighed in exasperation. "Cassie, you don't need your checkbook. I have the ranch checks and a line of credit authorization with me."

"I know." She didn't say another word, but concentrated on breathing. Casey looked out the side window at the dry landscape while she listened to the conversation between Ben and JD.

"Have you talked to Spencer since he accepted the developers' offer on their place, JD?"

"He can't wait to leave Colorado behind."

"Do you know what he's going to do?"

"I think he and Harrison are purchasing some farmland in Virginia adjacent to their grandparents place."

"Wouldn't you think he would want to keep some of the breeding stock that he's selling?"

JD shrugged and reached for his wife's hand. She seemed unusually quiet lately, like her mind was off in another world. Maybe all the questions during the investigation of Big Joe's car wreck had bothered her more that she let on. She'd told him it must have been divine intervention that sent him over the edge of the mountain at the same location where her family had died.

The list of persons interrogated had been extensive; it started with JD, Ben, Pete, Harlan, and Rick. Spencer, Harrison, and a dozen more, including the woman seated beside him, They had all been interviewed multiple times. An eternity passed before the toxicology reports came back. It was determined that Big Joe was driving under the influence and way over the legal limit for operating a vehicle. He had also ingested Valium prior to his demise. A prescription bottle of the tranquilizer was found in his desk at home and another, half empty, in the glove box of the mangled vehicle. Each of the primary suspects had witnesses to their whereabouts during the morning of the accident. His death was ruled accidental by the sheriff's department, the state troopers, and a multitude of insurance investigators.

JD was the one who talked Spencer into selling and starting fresh somewhere. His nephew was hell bent on burning down the house. He capitulated when JD warned him he could very well start a huge wildfire, dry as the area was, and it would provoke more inquiries by investigators.

******

Harlan and Tracy parked next to JD's crew cab. The others were left in the dust as Casey and Shadow hightailed it to locate a bathroom. Tracy followed in their wake, only to find Shadow standing guard outside a door off the utility room at the rear of the house. One look at Casey as she exited prompted Tracy to ask, "How far along are you?"

"I'm not sure. Everything has been so insane I've sort of lost track. My jeans felt overly snug this morning, and I had to fight with the zipper."

"Have you been ill before?"

"No, this is the first time. Whatever you do, Tracy, don't tell Harlan until I have a chance to clue JD in."

Fortunately, Harlan, and Spencer were in a huddle with Ben and JD when the women and Shadow returned. Casey noticed that George was absent. She found him on her way to register a bidding number of her own. He tagged along with her to look at some of the horses and tack that was to be auctioned.

Casey fell in love with a Paint weanling. The sorrel overo colt went home with her, along with a buggy, a sleigh, and a cute pair of Haflinger geldings. JD wasn't happy with her choices. He barely spoke on the return trip home, and she wondered about the private conversation that prompted JD to send George in search of her.

JD and Ben made five trips over the next two days, transporting the Angus breeding stock and a half-dozen, good-looking cowponies purchased for the combined ranches. He was still not communicating. Casey figured it wasn't what she bought, but the fact she spent her own money that annoyed him. She'd been making monetary decisions all of her adult life and was having trouble with being accountable to someone else.

On their return from driving George to the airport in Denver, she decided to tell her husband about her condition. She kept her eyes on the highway, and she fought not to white knuckle the steering wheel on her new, silver Yukon. "I have a doctor's appointment to keep tomorrow if you want to come along."

He glanced over toward the driver. "Are you asking me to go with you, Cassie?"

She figured since she was driving, he wouldn't strangle her for not telling him earlier. "Only if you want to. The doctor said she would do an ultrasound, and I thought you might want to get a first look at our son or daughter."

"I was wondering when you were going to break down and tell me you're pregnant, Cassie."

She thought Grandma Joan was probably smiling down on her little Cassandra and Jimmy Gannon. Joan was also getting a huge laugh out of Casey's surprise at her husband's keen awareness where she was concerned. Maybe in time she would be able to read him as well.

End

Meet the Author:

Ms. Anton is the author of the award winning children's series *Backyard Horse Tales*. In her 2015 award winning adult novel "Wind River Refuge" she turns her attention to the difficulties in overcoming childhood abuse. Set in the turbulent sixties and early seventies. This romance / who done it comes from a time before child advocacy, cell phones, and PCs.

Cassandra Hoffman begins her search for justice in the early decade of the twenty first century in Anton's latest adult novel Cassandra: Night Shades.

Please take a moment to review Casey's story. I love to hear from my readers, so drop me a line at talesbyjackie@yahoo.com. I will answer e-mails. Sign up for my Book of the Month Club and newsletter. Thank you for choosing Cassandra: Night Shades.

Additional Books by J.M.

2015 was the release of the first two books in the Troubles in Love-Land Series. Book One: "Fateful Waters" was released as an e-book and paperback May of 2015. Book Two: "Panhandle Mayhem" was be released November of 2015. There is more to come in the series for 2016.

Fateful Waters book trailer https://www.youtube.com/watch?v=H-5D2XAHzL0

The author lives in rural Ohio with her husband, two horses, two dogs, and abundant wildlife. Years of experience with horses and youth riders lend a unique perspective to her Backyard Horse Tales, and crop up in unexpected scenes in her adult works written with the pen name J.M.

Follow the authors writing blog or website for updates.

Writing Blog: http:"jackieanton.com/

Author Website: http:"talesbyjackie.com/

www.ingramcontent.com/pod-product-compliance
Lightning Source LLC
Chambersburg PA
CBHW020609300426
44113CB00007B/578